Real World Content Modeling
A Field Guide to CMS Features
and Architecture

by Deane Barker

Table of Contents

Introduction

When developing a content model, there are three challenges to overcome.

The first is understanding the value of a content model and what it can do for your organization. Most discussions about content modeling tend to concentrate on this question of "why"? We spend a lot of time explaining all the reasons we should model content in attempt to persuade someone a content model is a thing they need and should want.

This has already been done well. I'm going to let others keep fighting this battle.

But, once we've convinced people of the why, we run headlong into the second challenge: how do we actually create a model from a team and requirements standpoint? Meaning, how do we decide what types and attributes we need, and how should they all fit together?

This is a problem of discovery, analysis, team dynamics, trial and error, and dozens of other factors. Again, many resources have been written about this.

Assuming we know why we need a content model and assuming we've put together a good, logical plan, the challenge this guide is concerned with is the third one –

What tools do we actually have available to do this?

The answer to this one can be tricky. If you already have a CMS, then you have an existing toolset you need to work with, and it's helpful to know what modeling functionality that CMS offers before you start planning.

If you don't have a CMS and you need to acquire one, then knowing what tools you need helps inform the decision. Many teams don't know what features they should look for, or what questions they should ask when they go looking. They end up with a system which is completely mismatched to what they were trying to accomplish in the first place.

All too often, content models are developed according to abstract scenarios without any consideration of how they might be manifested in the (ahem) real world). Sadly, dreams of a perfectly matched model – and how it will benefit the organization – go out with window when the team realizes the system they have just won't support all the effort that went into planning the model.

I teach an "Introduction to Content Management" course to students in the Masters of Content Strategy degree program at FH Joanneum[1] in Graz, Austria. My course is in the last semester, and by the time the students get to me, they've been talking about content modeling for almost two years...from a content strategy perspective.

I open my lecture on content modeling roughly the same way every time:

> "I'm here to rain on your parade."

Why? Because, inevitably, you are limited by your tools. You can design the greatest house to ever be built, but if the only tools you have are dental floss and chewing gum, then you're never going to construct the home of your dreams. Likewise, you can plan the greatest content model in the world, but if all you have to manifest the model is an ancient CMS from back when rich text editing was a big deal, then a lot of your effort will be wasted.

Sometimes you have flexibility in CMS selection – "we're not going to pick a CMS that can't support what we want to do!" Other times, the CMS is set in stone – if your organization has seven figures into a vendor's solution, you can't swap it out just because it doesn't handle your model well. You may have to play the hand you were dealt.

Whenever I evaluate a CMS, I first try to figure out how it models content in

---

1. *This is one of the few degree programs in content strategy available in the world. https://www.fh-joanneum.at/content-strategie-und-digitale-kommunikation/master/en/ programme/*

general and what specific modeling features are available. I believe, above anything else a CMS does, how it models content is foundational – both for an obvious reason, and a subtle one.

First, and obviously, the tools a CMS offers for content modeling are critical to building a good content model. As I said before, if you don't have a decent hammer, building a house is going to be difficult.

Second, and less obviously, the tools a CMS offers for content modeling *are usually an accurate predictor of the quality of the rest of the system.*

Content modeling is so fundamental that if a CMS screws that up, there's a very good chance other parts of the system fall short as well. Content modeling is the gatekeeper to determine if the team who architected the system had any idea of what they were doing.

I've seen systems so deficient in basic modeling capabilities, that I just knew the rest of the system was going to be hopelessly flawed as well. Perhaps it was a self-fulfilling prophecy, but that initial impression never failed me.

CMS capabilities operate on a *wide* range. There are some commonalities, certainly, but beyond the basics, different systems offer a lot of different tools. Some are fantastic if you can find them, and others are superfluous or can be improvised by creative use of other features.

And small variations in how a feature is implemented can cause wide variations in usability and applicability. A seemingly minor change in implementation can cause a gaping functional chasm when trying to put the feature into practice. Sadly, by the time enough layers have been peeled off for these differences to become apparent, the software has been purchased, half-implemented, and there's no going back.

What I think has been missing over the years is a comprehensive survey of the features and capabilities that different CMSs offer to allow content to be modeled.

This guide is an attempt to be that missing feature survey. I've worked with a lot of systems over the years and taken particular note of how they model content. What I've tried to assemble here is a broad view of everything I've observed in the market, and how these features might relate to common content modeling problems and scenarios.

The goal of this guide is to increase your fluency and ability to ask the right questions. Half of the problem with evaluating software is knowing the breadth of what's possible. The only way to know where an option exists on the scale of competency is to understand the range and outer limits of the scale. You can't decide what's "good" or "bad" without knowing what those terms even mean in an absolute sense.

About this Guide

I started writing this guide one Sunday morning before church. It was supposed to be a blog post. A few months prior, I wrote a post about the lack of a modeling standard in CMS, which got quite a bit of traction.

This eventually led to a conference call with some very smart people about what we might do as an industry to move forward. It got me thinking perhaps someone should just write a draft standard (because *nothing* gets people talking productively like a concrete thing they can criticize).

The original idea of this guide was to paint a picture of what a standard might look like. My goal was to promote some level of interoperability, so that content systems might acquire some degree of similarity at a base level. The hope was that this would make it easier for systems to exchange content.

However, a few thousand words in, it became apparent that I was completely wrong with how I approached it. For interoperability, we'd need to standardize the *external interface* of a model, while what I was writing was about the *internal implementation* of the model. (I address this more deeply in the postscript.)

And by the time I realized that, I was having a lot of fun talking about content modeling feature implementation, so decided to ride that theme for a while. Many tens of thousands of words later, here we are.

There are a few audiences who might find this guide helpful.

- **Customers** evaluating a specific CMS or embarking on a market search. This guide attempts to explain, in the broadest possible terms, the full range of modeling features you might find in the market. If you have no idea what questions you should ask or what features you should look for, this guide will help.

- **Content strategists** tasked with developing content models for a variety of target CMSs. Knowing how different systems might manifest the content models you create can help you understand an existing CMS or educate your clients about what features they might need in a future CMS.

- **Vendors** initially developing a new CMS or continuing to develop an existing CMS. Perspective is good, and it's helpful to see what features and capabilities exist in other systems.

- **Architects and developers** who want to better understand the genre of tools they work with every day.

- **CMS geeks** who just want to talk about CMS all day long. You know who you are, and *I feel you.*

Some parts of this guide are web specific, which doesn't mean we're ignorant of headless and enterprise content management branches of this industry.

Addressing the peculiarities of *web* CMS is unavoidable for two reasons:

- Like it or not, web content management (WCM or WCMS) is a huge part of this industry and will be for the foreseeable future. Yes, headless applications are growing, but the industry is still dominated by web-specific platforms.

- Web content management is a superset of other flavors of content management. A web system needs everything a headless system offers... *and then some more stuff.* So, in discussing WCMS concepts, nothing was ignored in the headless or enterprise CMS space. This guide still covers all that functionality, it just adds the web-specific concepts on top.

If your application isn't web specific, you're free to skip those parts. It's not a lot of extra, however, so read it for some perspective and because you might find those parts more applicable than you think.

The content management industry has no central, governing authority, so we lack an accepted vocabulary – not for lack of effort; see The Web Content Management Glossary[1].

For this reason, there's a few things to be aware of when reading this guide:

- For accepted concepts known by different names, I had to pick a term and go with it. "Type" is used rather than a "template" or a "class" (sorry Sitecore, sorry eZ Publish). "Attribute" is used rather than a "property" or a "field" (sorry Episerver, sorry Drupal).

- For more amorphous concepts, I simply had to invent terms. There are things we talk about and around in this industry that no one really puts a definitive name on, or they might be named in other contexts, but they're not CMS-specific. When this happens, please just roll with it and know that I'm not trying to stake an intellectual claim when I make up nomenclature, but rather putting some semantic boundaries around a concept to make it easier to discuss.

A couple other notes about language and terminology:

I believe the plural of "CMS" is "CMS." The "S" can stand for either "system" or "systems." However, for my first book[2], I was over-ruled by my editor. I've complained about this publicly[3], but have come to accept grammatical purity is trumped by common understanding, so "CMSs" it will be.

The word "system" is used a lot. In almost all contexts, this means the same as "CMS."

Finally, this guide is explaining general principles spread across many different software platforms (again, like my first book). With this in mind, I will exhaust all sorts of qualifiers (e.g., many, most, some, often, sometimes).

I hope they're accurate (i.e., "most" should always mean more often than "some"), but take them for the vague qualifiers than they are.

When you discuss content modeling deeply enough, you'll inevitably start to drift across discipline boundaries. Beyond modeling, for example, I touch on the following disciplines in this guide:

- Interface design
- Information architecture

---

1. *"The Web Content Management Glossary." http://flyingsquirrelbook.com/glossary/*
2. *"Web Content Management: Systems, Features, and Best Practices." http://flyingsquirrelbook.com/*
3. *"The Plural of CMS." https://flyingsquirrelbook.com/notes/12/the-plural-of-cms/*

- Database design
- Web protocols
- General programming
- Development operations ("dev ops")

I try to call this out when it happens and pull back before falling too far into the weeds when crossing boundaries to explain a concept. My hope is your eyes don't glaze over before I get back on track, but no promises.

The same is true of other domains of functionality within a CMS itself. By the time you finish this document, we'll have covered quite a bit of ground about CMS architecture and functionality. As you read, know we are adhering as close as possible to the disciplines of content modeling.

For example, here are things we're not going to cover *directly*:

- Editorial workflow and tools
- Content optimization
- Templating
- Multi-channel delivery
- Analytics

There's *something* about all of those disciplines in the coming pages, but only as they relate to content modeling. Entire books have been written about each of them, but we're only concerned with how they might intersect with the ways a CMS supports a content model.

The "reverse pyramid" model of journalism says a story should start with the most general concepts and get more and more specific, so a reader can quit without finishing and still walk away with the most important information.

I tried to follow this model. This guide gets progressively deeper and more esoteric as we go.

There are a lot of chapters, and they're short. Each one is dedicated to a specific feature or concept. They will start with the most basic questions and move down the list to features that are more uncommon and specialized.

Occasionally, I'll take a "timeout" to discuss a general concept that doesn't quite rise to the level of pure evaluation, but is helpful to understand for context.

At the end of most chapters are some evaluation questions you can ask system vendors to help understand their capabilities, or ask *yourself* to test and guide your understanding of your own system.

Please don't "weaponize" this list by aggregating it and dumping it on vendors. These are tools for discussion and discovery, not demands.

The earlier chapters were easier to write. Basic content modeling features are common enough to have developed accepted conventions around. However, as the functionality got more and more advanced, some of it got harder to write. When discussing a feature not in every system, I started having to take more leaps.

In most cases, I'm describing features I have actually seen. In other cases, I realized I wasn't describing a feature I had observed as much as I was describing a feature or architecture that made sense to me in a perfect world. If everyone did everything correctly, this is how this *should* work and wouldn't that be great?

Occasionally, I thought I remembered some particular functionality from a specific system, then, upon further research, discovered I was misremembering it. However, the feature would have been *fantastic* if my memory had been accurate. I discuss those mythical features too, in the perhaps vain hope all my functional dreams will come true one day.

In other situations, I frame functionality as questions to which there might not be a valid answer. Some logical situations present paradoxes and intricacies that can't easily be solved with technology, so some questions are simply open-ended and left to you to relate to your own situation.

This leads to the inescapable point: *no one system will embody everything in this guide*. If you're looking for a system that does everything here, you're going to be disappointed.

Some systems do more than others. In this guide, I have the freedom of both piecing together the best parts of every system I've ever seen, and then extending that by describing a hypothetically perfect system *no one has ever seen*. This guide is both realistic and theoretical at the same time.

More than anything, my ultimate goal was to introduce questions and paradigms of thinking about modeling solutions that expand your perspective on the discipline.

How a CMS Helps (Or Hinders) Your Content Model

As I mentioned, I'm not going to go deep into *why* we create content models. This guide assumes you already understand why you need a content model and the value it brings. What we're going to talk about in this chapter are the principles of a model that a CMS can make better or worse, depending on the features it offers (or doesn't) and their relative competency.

But first, some theory.

Content modeling is the accumulative adding of value to raw data.

In my masters course, I define information as "data with context." We take raw data and – in a gross over-simplification – we put labels on it.

"3" is a datum.

It's clearly a digit that exists on the numeric scale. We know it's more than "2" and less than "4" but we don't know anything else about it.

- It could be the number of ice cream cones I ate last week.
- It could be the number of U.S. Supreme Court justices who attended Harvard.

- It could be the number of children I have.

In fact, it's that last one (I didn't eat any ice cream cones last week, and five of the nine current SCOTUS justices attended Harvard).

By putting a label on this, we've moved from a raw datum to information:

- Number of children Deane has: 3

This datum now has interpretive value. You can draw personal judgments about what this means about me and my family situation. And you can relate it to other values, like the average number of children of the American family and draw judgments about what this means.

Information is data with labels. Something as simple as a label adds context – "the circumstances surrounding the thing."

We can add even more information to a datum in ways other than just labeling – we can do it by adding structure.

What if we had a list of text strings labeled "Names of Deane's Children in Descending Order by Age"?

- Alec

- Gabrielle

- Isabella

By creating some structure, we've further increased the value of raw data. Now, in addition to knowing the number of children I have, we know their names and in what order they arrived.

How do we know their names and the order they arrived? *Because that's the label we put on it.* The label isn't just decoration. Rather, we're explicitly establishing some context for this data. We're telling the information consumer what this thing is. We could change the label to "Deane's Pets" and now it would mean something different.

As obvious as this sounds, *things are what we say they are.*

Our CMS helps us maintain this structure. It can give me a little editing widget to "Add a new child," and it can reject my entry if I leave it blank.

This type of modeling is discrete, meaning it's wholly contained in a single object. We can do this relationally as well. If we're working with content type called Person, we could define a property called "Spouse."

- [reference to a content object representing Annie Barker]

By modeling that relationship, we can now traverse our content model. We've created a graph, and we can transition from one object to another with some idea of how they relate. That link creates value in itself – not only does it identify the other object, but by virtue of the label, you also know how we relate. The property isn't called "Dentist," it's called "Spouse," and that gives you more information.

Since this is a link, perhaps our repository system can offer me a "content finder" to go looking for Annie's content object.

As my life progresses, our content model gives us some resiliency. For instance, bigamy laws being what they are, we might enforce a validation rule ensuring I can only have one link marked "Spouse" at any one time, to ensure I don't have two of them.

All of this content exists inside an information system of some kind. It's only as good as it can be represented and modeled *inside that system* – how we can label it, structure it, and work with it over time. The functionality that systems provide for this exists on a wide scale, and is the subject of this guide.

What the last section intended to illustrate are the four principles of a content model that the features of a CMS have a direct impact on:

- **Descriptiveness**: A content model is fundamentally a *description* of content. A CMS helps or hinders the quality of this description. A poor CMS will make our description crude and low-fidelity. A good CMS gives us the ability to paint a more accurate picture about what our content is and what it should be used for.

- **Usability**: A content model is only as good as the content that goes into it, and an editor's ability to create good content is deeply dependent on the tools they have to work with. A good CMS will use the defined model to offer optimized interfaces that encourage editors to create quality content.

- **Resiliency**: A content model that's perfect in theory can be quickly destroyed by a CMS that doesn't protect it. A poor CMS will allow editors to violate the rules of the model – the model is said to be **brittle**. A good CMS will prevent content from being created or edited in an invalid state, so other people and processes interacting with the content can trust it's a stable and predictable format. (One could almost call this principle **predictability**, since the goal of resiliency is content that doesn't deviate from the expected model.)

- **Manageability**: A content model might be complex, and it will usually always change over time. A poor CMS encourages bad management practices that turn an initially perfect model into a jumbled mess. A good CMS can help a content strategist, editor, or administrator maintain their model; keep its definitions clear, concise, and understandable; and make changes orderly, precise, and predictable.

The four concepts comprise the core of what content modeling is. It's the process of –

1. Enriching data by putting labels and structure around it

2. Configuring the CMS to allow it to assist editors when working with it

3. Enforcing rules to prevent content from existing in an invalid state

4. Keeping this clear and understandable, both on initial launch and over time

Since the raw data isn't known in advance, content modeling is the creation of a framework of rules on which to "hang" future data to provide more value. It's like city planning – you design a structure for maximum use and future value, then watch as your city grows into it.

Again, these aspects are not about the design of content model itself. The competency of the model is an independent variable – you can still come up with a terrible content model, even if it's implemented in the world's most capable CMS.

However, the competency of the model isn't under consideration here. We're assuming you had the assistance of a competent content strategist who designed a content model to fit your needs.

All we're concerned about within this guide are the CMS tools to support whatever model is specified, measured by how those tools contribute to the four core principles.

The discussion of a rules framework inside which content "grows" has me thinking about SimCity, which was one of my favorite video games for years.

SimCity is a game about city planning. You develop infrastructure – streets, power plants, zoning rules, etc. – and then your computer people grow a city inside that framework. As this city grows, you need to adapt your infrastructure to accommodate what they do. You need to add new streets, increase power output, find new ways to deliver water, etc.

I loved this idea of guiding an autonomous and growing system of interactions. I used to set up infrastructure, watch the city grow, then reset the game, adjust my infrastructure, and start it again to watch how the "people" would react and adjust. I was fascinated by complexity theory before I even knew what that was.

Over the course of this guide, I hope you'll come to see the parallels for your content model. You are defining the rules of the content game for your editors by using the tools of your CMS to keep them safe and serve them effectively. You goal is to use these rules to allow them to thrive.

The Anatomy of a Content Model

For the purposes of this guide, we need to baseline what the technical underpinnings of a content model consist of. We'll add a lot more definitions throughout this guide, but we first need to establish the basics.

And just to reiterate a disclaimer – most of these concepts go by other names in different contexts and platforms. Since we need to standardize some names, this is what we're going with.

Fair warning: some of this chapter might seem complex and even pedantic. But push through, because what's in here will set a foundation for the concepts we discuss in the remainder of this guide.

When we discussed theory in the last chapter we made the point that content is just a set of labeled data. We take a datum and "wrap" it in a label and some other context so we can describe it, manipulate it, and refer to it.

This construct is called an **attribute**.

An attribute is a logical container – a "bundle" – holding lots of parts that work together.

- The actual datum – the thing we're managing – is the **attribute value**.

- The attribute will have an internal **name** of some kind. This is a unique identifier the system uses to differentiate this attribute from any other. It usually has to be in a machine-friendly format, which means restrictions on casing (usually lower), spacing (usually none), and limits on non-alphanumeric characters (sometimes none, but occasionally underscores) – something like `title` or `ageInYears`. And as we'll discuss in a later chapter, this name might be unchangeable once set.

- The attribute will usually also have a more user-friendly **label** for display to editors. This is intended for human consumption, and it's critical for usability. Many times, it's just the name with appropriate capitalization ("Title"), but it can also be more descriptive ("Age (in years)").

- The attribute will need to be stored in an underlying data management system, which is usually a relational database. This means the attribute is mapped to a primitive **datatype** such as a series of characters, a number, or a date.

- Depending on the system, the attribute will often have a **typed value** representation, which is how the attribute value is represented in the underlying programming language.

- The attribute will often have some **serialization** and **deserialization** code to convert the primitive datatype value to and from its typed value.

- The attribute will usually have **editorial element** to allow human editors to create and edit the value. Sometimes this is a simple input field, but some editorial elements are a complex interface of multiple fields and controls.

- The attribute will often have one or more **validation rules** which prevent the value from being stored unless it meets specified criteria

That's clearly a lot. As a CMS editor, you likely won't ever see an attribute broken down to this level.

These different parts always exist, but they're often just implied, assumed, and spread out across different subsystems so you never see them all in aggregate. Even a developer might not interact with all the different parts of an attribute, since only a subset might require customization or configuration at any one time (if customization is even offered), so most of this stays under the covers.

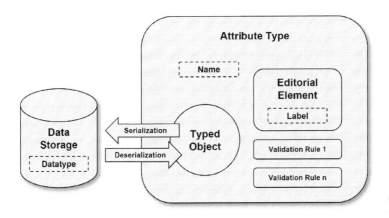

A simplistic representation of all the different parts making up a single attribute inside a CMS.

The unique combination of everything described above is an attribute type. These are all the pieces that work together to manage data as an attribute *when assigned to a content type*, which we'll talk about below.

Attributes don't exist in isolation, meaning you'll never have an attribute just floating around all by itself. Instead, they are grouped together into **content types**.

A content type is a set of attributes which combine to describe a logical unit of content. An Article is a type, which is comprised of a set of attributes – Title, Body, etc.

A type does not contain any actual data. *All data is contained in attributes.* A type is just a way to organize multiple attributes into a usable aggregation.

Like an attribute, a type has a name and a label, with the same purpose and limitations as an attribute. The **name** is how the system refers to the type, and the **label** is for human consumption.

Other than that, a type contains comparatively little inherent information. There might be a few settings, like permissions or other system-specific information, but types are generally just a wrapper boundary around attributes.

Content Type

Name   Label

Attribute Assignment 1   Settings   Type

Attribute Assignment n   Settings   Type

The basic concept of a type as a wrapper around a collection of attributes. Types don't contain much inherent information themselves. They generally just serve as a reusable collection of attributes.

Note that attribute types might carry assignment-specific settings, depending on the system. So the behavior of the attributes is the combination of its (1) type, and (2) settings for that specific assignment.

Article Page   ⑦

A page representing a dated set of narrative information.

Information

Name   Article
Display name   Article Page

⚙ Settings

⚙ Add Property

		Name	Field name	Type	Required	Localized	Searchable	Tab
	⬇	Body	Main Body	XHTML string (>255)	Yes	Yes	Yes	Content
⬆	⬇	Author	Author(s)	String (<= 255)	Yes		Yes	Content
⬆		Category	Category Assignment	Category selection				Content

A visual example of a page type in Episerver. This type has three explicit attributes (called "Properties" in Episerver) – Body, Author, and Category. There is no explicit title because the built-in model of Episerver content includes a name. Note too that in Episerver, what we referred to as an attribute label is called the "Field name."

Episerver attribute assignments have settings which govern their behavior (localized, searchable, etc.), but these settings cannot be saved and re-used.

Types would necessarily need to contain at least one attribute. Remember that types don't carry any data themselves, so if they didn't contain at least one attribute, they wouldn't have a reason to exist. (Note that a type might have a built-in attribute which carries data, which we'll talk about soon.)

The assignment of an attribute type to a content type is many-to-many, meaning assigning an attribute with the type of "Text" to the Article type and calling it Title now creates a single assignment – the Title on Article is *not* the same as the Title on Employee Profile. The term **attribute assignment** refers to the instance of an attribute assigned to a type.

Technically, when we talk about an "attribute" in the context of it existing on a type, we should always say "attribute assignment," because we're talking about a specific attribute type assigned to a specific content type with a specific name. However, this is awkward, so we'll use the less semantically-pure option and just say "attribute."

The assignment of an attribute usually allows **assignment settings** to govern the behavior of *that* attribute on *that* content type. Occasionally, a system will allow you to save these settings and reuse the resulting combination of type and settings multiple times.

Finally, a content type is a *unique* combination of attributes. Could you have two content types, both with the exact same collection of attributes? Yes...but what would be the point? If two types have the exact same collection of attribute types with the exact same settings, then they are functionally the same type.

> I can imagine a few cases (*very* few) where doing this makes sense. You might call the two types something different – Article and Blog Post, for example – and you might gain some differentiation from naming (you might have some different rules for one over the other), but that would likely be extremely confusing to editors.
>
> Suffice that in most cases, a specific combination of attributes constitutes a specific type, which is unique from all other types.

Discussions of types and attributes are just talking about an empty *model* with no content in it. When we start adding data, we move from a content type to a **content object**.

Types and attributes (and, really, our entire content model) is just a cookie cutter. It's a pattern, like a utensil for shaping cookies into a star or a snowman. When we start creating content, we start stamping out cookie after cookie in the same shape. We might have a million content *objects* of a single type.

This is a *very important* distinction to make. When I say "type," I mean the pattern, template, or cookie cutter. This is the "plan" for content. When I say "object," I mean actual content created from that type.

> This concept of types being templates for actual content goes all the way back to Plato's Theory of Forms[7]. Plato believed everything in the real world was an instance of a more ideal concept or "form." The table in your dining room is a representation of the universal idea of "table-ness" that exists only in theory.
>
> > These Forms are the essences of various objects: they are that without which a thing would not be the kind of thing it is. [...] Plato's Socrates held that the world of Forms is transcendent to our own world (the world of substances) and also is the essential basis of reality. Super-ordinate to matter, Forms are the most pure of all things.
>
> Heady stuff, to be sure, but the parallels are clear. I'll give bonus points to the first CMS with the guts to refer to content types as "Platonic Forms."

We will discuss types and attributes so often in the coming chapters that I've highlighted them background shading to differentiate them from other text.

1. *The Wikipedia page on Plato's theory. https://en.wikipedia.org/wiki/Theory_of_forms*

Evaluation Criteria #1

What is the built-in content model?

In college, I read a textbook about communication that said:

> There is no opposite of communication. You can't *not* communicate anything because even the absence of communication in itself communicates something.

The same is true of a content model. A CMS can't *not* have a content model. If it stores content in any way (which it would have to, being a "CMS" and all), then it has to store it according to some rules and structure, no matter how simplistic.

Consider a wiki. The most basic wiki in the world has two fields: (1) a title, and (2) a body of text.

Editing Content management system

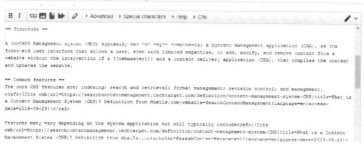

This is the editor for Wikipedia. While it allows a lot of sometimes confusing markup, it is fundamentally a two-element content model – title and body – and you aren't even allowed to change the title post-publish (you have to "move" the page).

Simple as it is, a wiki has content model. What you type in the Title field is the...title, and what you type in the Body field is the...body. The title isn't the body and the body isn't the title, and we know this because there's a declared model behind it. Simple as it is, those two things are distinct, named attributes.

We'll call this the **built-in model**. This is the model the CMS uses internally, and enforces at some level.

It's common for most systems to require every object to have a Name or Title attribute. Often, every content type gets that by default. Many systems will also have another text field for Body or Content or Text. While it stores characters just like the Title it's generally a larger field, accommodating more text, such as a raw textarea or a rich text editor.

The easiest way to discuss a content model is to visualize the editorial interface, because, in most cases, all the attributes of a built-in model are reflected in the user interface (UI).

The main editing interface for the early blogging platform Movable Type. You can see a more typical model here, one specific to the idea of a "blog post." You have a Title, a Body, some keywords, and checkboxes to change the behavior in various ways.

In addition to the Title and Body, the Movable Type interface above also shows some built-in attributes that might get classified as "metadata," or "data about data," which we'll talk about in the next chapter. These are attributes such as:

- Publication Status
- Publish Date
- URL Segment ("Basename" in the image above)
- Categorization
- Change Note/Comment

These are properties that will never display to the public – so they won't be directly consumed by a human – but which exist to change the behavior of the content.

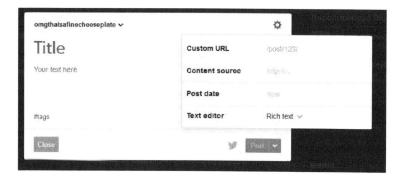

Tumblr offers just a title, text, and tags in the default interface. The gear icon pops out a menu with some additional information.

Now, remember back to our discussion of theory – our simple wiki content model and the default Tumblr model shown above still provide us with some benefit:

1. We have names and labels, so we can separate the Title from the Body

2. We can tell the editing interface that the Title should be a single-line textbox, and the Body should be a multiline textarea (perhaps even a rich text editor)

3. We can ensure that every content object has a Title by refusing to create or update an object unless a Title has been entered

So no matter how simple, a content model gives us some advantages.

Knowing the built-in model is helpful because you need to know what you have to work with and how you might need to extend it. Additionally, knowing the built-in model gives you some insight into functionality – if a system is managing Start Publish and Stop Publish dates, then it clearly allows scheduled publishing and expiration; if it manages URL Segment, then it must allow URL management.

In most every situation, the built-in model won't encompass all of your requirements, and you'll need to change or extend it. Let's talk now about whether/how that's possible.

Evaluation Questions

- What is the built-in model – what content types are in the product as installed, and what attributes do they possess?

Timeout

What's the difference between built-in and custom?

You'll see a dichotomy in the upcoming chapters between **built-in** and **custom**.

Any CMS comes "out of the box" with a specific featureset, but many systems let you enable new functionality to suit your specific situation. Developers can usually enable this functionality by writing code against specific **application programming interfaces** (API) – provided by the CMS.

An API is a collection of "access points" in the CMS where external developers (meaning, *your* developers, not the developers who created the CMS) can attach their own code to fit the CMS to their specific situation. A good API is one that's clear, logical, and provides sufficient attachment points for developers. A poor API is one that's unnecessarily complicated, confusing, and/or doesn't provide access to the features a developer wants to work with.

Unfortunately, the line between what's built-in and what's custom gets blurry and is idiosyncratic to the system, because what one system considers basic configuration would be considered wildly custom by another.

For example, some systems are modeled from programming code, and this is completely expected and not considered custom. Other systems are modeled from a user interface (UI), and if anyone is writing code, then they're doing something custom.

There might also be a dichotomy between **code** and **configuration**. Custom code usually means executable, programming code in the language of the CMS itself that executes in the same process. Changing code usually involves a complete redeployment of the CMS to the production environment. Configuration is anything short of code, which can mean changing text in some structured markup file (XML or YAML, for instance), or clicking your way through a provided interface.

What is custom, in relation to a specific CMS? It could be a change that –

- Is created in an underlying programming language of the CMS itself, and which executes in the same computing process
- Involves file configuration that has to be deployed to the production environment
- Cannot be completed from the administrative interface
- Prevents the system from being automatically upgraded
- Requires a developer to complete
- Requires the production computing process to be restarted
- Requires testing in a separate environment

And some of these definitions just raise more questions and need for more definitions –

- What is a "developer" in the context of this system?
- What is a "deployment"?
- What is an "environment"?

I'm not even going to try to answer or define those, because they're hopelessly specific to whatever system you're working with. For example, some systems don't have environments at all, which deeply affects what we might call a deployment.

In the end, what's "custom" is often based on the expectations of the system.

Each system has a level of expected development to implement it. Anything over and above that development is some vary degree of "custom" ranging from mild to heroic. Some systems are designed to be extended – they come with multiple extension points and a well-documented API – while other systems are hermetically sealed.

It's just not an exact definition. I'll try to make the distinction clear when it comes up, but know the dichotomy is very much relative to your particular CMS and its implementation patterns.

Evaluation Questions

- What is the primary method of model extension – custom code or configuration?
- If configuration, is that through structured data files which are deployed, or through the administrative UI?

Evaluation Criteria #2

Can the built-in model be extended with custom content types?

Given every system has a built-in content model, can you extend this to create your own content types? From a modern perspective, you might think, "well, of course...", but this isn't always automatic, especially with older systems and systems designed for specific use cases.

Some systems are designed to be extended, and, in fact, would be fairly useless if *not* extended. These systems have a stripped-down built-in model because they intend it simply as a starting point. These systems have many built-in attribute types, and an expected part of development is for you to define the content model and new types to fit your situation.

Other systems allow extensions grudgingly, perhaps offering the ability to add some "custom fields" that only store text and cannot be validated. These systems might have a rich built-in model which is often meant to serve the needs of a particular use case for which the software was designed. These systems likely maintain some glimmer of hope that their built-in model won't need to be extended at all.

> Real Story Group has called this the difference between "products" and "platforms."[1]

Other systems simply don't allow any model extension. They are what they are. These systems are usually subscription-based or meant solely to service some particular use case (which is the subject of the next chapter).

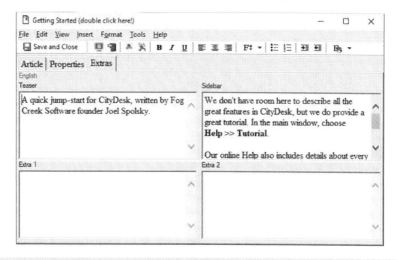

CityDesk was an early, desktop-based CMS. You can see here on the "extras" tab that it had some usage-appropriate attributes, and two special attributes – Extra 1 and Extra 2 – which we designed to hold...whatever. And this was it. If you needed an Extra 3 you were out of luck, or you had to just re-use one of the existing fields.

In some systems, there is a distinction between **content** and **metadata**. The former is what you're actually managing, and the latter is...other stuff. It's like the opening act and the headliner at a music concert. You came for the headliner; the opening act is just extra.

This model is more easily illustrated in the document management space – these are systems that manage files (Word, PDF, etc.) and allow you to store other data *about* those files.

When you have a file you're managing, *the file is the thing*, and the metadata

---

1. *"How the New Platforms vs. Products Debate Impacts Your Success".* https://www.re-alstorygroup.com/Library/Download/43

is...extra. You're clearly managing the file as the content. The metadata is just extra information that enhances the data in the document.

Some early CMSs follow this same model, as they were just thin wrappers around rich text editors that generated chunks of HTML, or files that contained HTML. The idea was editors would edit the HTML content, and they would enhance it with metadata to provide organization and structure around it.

In these systems, the metadata was separate from the HTML content. So, the content was the content, and the "metadata" was...extra.

Serena Collage was a CMS-ish wrapper around a traditional source-code management system – imagine if someone turned Git into a CMS.

As such, an actual, versioned HTML file was the thing you were managing, and your only ability to add structure was to add "metadata" around this file. Collage had a dialog box where you could specify additional information to connected to the file and used in other contexts, like lists of content. *The file was the thing*, and the metadata was...extra.

(Note: I tried very hard to find a screencap of this, but Collage is a system in rare usage these days. Multiple requests and retweets on Twitter could not produce a working instance of it anywhere.)

Other file-based systems have used the idea of a "sidecar file" which is a file sitting alongside the "content file" which provides metadata that can't be stored with the file. If the actual content is in "article.html", a file next to it named "article.info" might store the metadata. The CMS knows to look for this file-naming structure for the metadata associated with content.

Ektron (acquired by Episerver in 2015) separated the concept of "content" and "meta-data." For a long time, "content" was just rich text – the "Content" tab in the image is just a "what you see is what you get" (WYSIWYG) editor. When Ektron wanted to add the idea of extendable, structured content, they put it in a separate tab. So your content was unstructured rich text, and your metadata was extendable, structured data.

The content/metadata dichotomy is less relevant today. The days of managing content as big chunks of HTML are (thankfully) mostly behind us, and most content has a higher degree of structure.

And this brings us to the awkward question of whether metadata in the classic sense even exists anymore.

Here's the definition of the prefix "meta":

> A prefix added to the name of a subject and designating another subject that analyzes the original one but at a more abstract, higher level

So, the word "metadata" literally means "data about data." The idea was the metadata was used as a tool to organize, clarify, or filter the "main" data. This means that to say something is metadata is to tacitly admit it's modifying some other data, which exists somewhere else.

Metadata only has meaning as a concept if it's separate from some other data. Refer back to the document management scenario and it makes more sense because the document is "the thing" and the metadata is "the other thing."

But what if there's no document or big chunk of HTML? What if there's no *thing*?

Put another way, what if everything is metadata? If everything is metadata, then *nothing* is. There is no "other."

The truth is that with most modern CMSs, the idea of "metadata" doesn't exist. All data is structured, and it's lumped into the same interface.

> Even if there's no metadata in CMS, this does give me a chance to mention there's some great "meta" in pop culture. Some TV shows, in particular, are legendary for meta references where the show acknowledges it's really a bunch of actors performing a script. *Arrested Development* and *Community*, in particular, were famous for this.

Let's come back to the original question: can the built-in content model be extended at all?

The *lack* of this ability is rare, but if you cannot extend the built-in model, then you need to be absolutely convinced it will do everything you need, both now and in the future. These situations are not common, and usually only exist in unapologetically use case-specific systems like those created for a particular industry vertical.

Assuming we *can* extend the built-in model, let's find out what attribute building blocks we have available.

Evaluation Questions

- Is it an expectation that the built-in model will be customized and extended by those implementing the system?
- Can new content types be configured?
- Is there an explicit difference between content and metadata?

Timeout

Opinionated Software

From our current perspective, limits on the extension of a built-in model might seem incredibly simplistic and self-defeating. And it is, but this introduces us to the concept of **opinionated software**.

With all software, you're very much bounded by the target use case that software was designed for, and, by extension, the opinions of the development team that built it. What *they* think is a good idea is passed down to you, and hopefully you think it's a good idea too. You don't get an opinion other than the one they give you.

Some software is a platform on which you can build anything. Other software is designed to do a specific thing. The former tends to allow a wide range of customization, while the latter allows a much narrower range. Indeed, some software is designed to do something so specific that the developers have imbued it with extremely strong opinions of how it should be used, and you can't easily overcome those opinions to get it to do anything else.

Why would anyone agree to this? Because if your opinions *do* actually line up with theirs, then it can make your life easier.

What if someone designed a software system to work for the exact usage scenario you have, in the exact way you think it should work, and no other way? Those are some strong opinions, but if they line up perfectly with yours, then everything is fine.

And this is the crux of opinionated software. Your affection for it is directly proportional to how closely its opinions line up with yours.

All software is opinionated to some extent, the only question is how strong those opinions are. It's a spectrum.

Strongly opinionated software tends to thrive in industry verticals. For example, museums have a sub-genre of content management called "Collection Management" which is used to manage all the information related to items in their collections. These systems are quite opinionated, which works because managing a museum collection is a specialized practice, around which a lot of patterns have developed. In scenarios like these, there's a better chance the development team's opinions will line up with the user's.

Beyond industry verticals, almost all content usage falls into patterns. Let's consider the common requirement to display a list of pages. Here are some of the patterns you might see:

- Each entry in the list of pages displays the title which is linked to a dedicated URL for that page

- The title of each entry is accompanied by a summary and perhaps a date

- The list can be ordered by a specified attribute (often Date Published or something similar); this order can ascend or descend

- Each entry in the list displays an image in a standard alignment and size, also linked to the dedicated URL for that page

- The list is paginated to a set number of entries per page, with page navigation links at the bottom

Make no mistake – this list is, in itself, a set of opinions of what you might need to do with a list of web pages. But in my experience, these are a pretty mainstream set of opinions. (And, yes, that statement is also an opinion.) A system might provide the capabilities of this list as base functionality, and those features would likely satisfy a significant percentage of customers.

Does this list of features address *your* specific use case? If so, perfect. If not, you have a few options:

1. Customize your implementation using the tools provided by the system

2. Find a different system that gives you the features you need

3. *Change your use case*

That last one is more common than you might think. Often the evaluation of a system involves some level of "requirements settling," where the purchaser is aware the opinions of the system don't totally match up with their use cases. Since it's good enough in other areas, and the concessions they need to make aren't huge, they just settle for what it offers, adjusting their plans and expectations to match.

Ideally, however, you usually want CMS software to be generalized. The trend in the market – above the very low end – is for platforms on which you can build or configure a more specific set of functionality to serve your individual situation. In these cases, fewer opinions are better.

Here's a dynamic that's often true, but few customers will confess to: some customers *want* a piece of software to enforce its opinions.

I've seen this in the intranet space quite a bit – intranet usage falls into very common patterns, and many intranet managers want both a system to manage their intranets, and opinions on *how* to manage it. An "intranet in a box" is an attractive product for many organizations, because it promises to deliver both practical functionality and a suggested model of usage.

Many customers look at software vendors as some of the most experienced practitioners in their field, and these customers consider a software product to come with a bundle of built-in, hard-won consulting. They take comfort in this.

There's often an unconscious bias to think the way packaged software does things is correct, and if it doesn't do something, then that thing didn't need to be done. Vendors are selling both a software product *and* a philosophy/methodology for its usage and the practice area it addresses, and for some customers, this is exactly what they want.

Evaluation Questions

- Is the system designed primarily for any specific vertical that might dictate the content model it supports?

- Is the system designed primarily to publish content to a specific channel – web, mobile, etc.? What opinions does it enforce on that channel?

Evaluation Criteria #3

What built-in attribute types are available?

Content types consist of a unique combination of attributes. If you can extend your content model to create new content types, you need to know what attributes types are available. They are the blocks with which you build your model. Without them, you have nowhere to start.

Each attribute, remember, is a container or label for a raw datum. The attribute has a name to identify what it represents – Title, Body, Date Published, whatever – and it also has a type which governs its behavior – what it can store, and how it appears to editors.

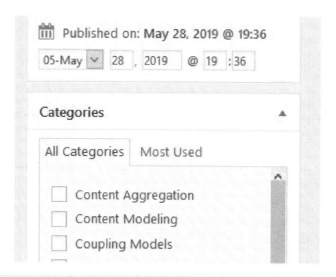

Two attributes in the WordPress interface, both storing different types of data with different editorial elements. Published stores a data value from a series of selection elements, and Categories stores multiple assignment references from a series of checkboxes.

Content falls into patterns, and every CMS that allows content model extension will provide a "menu" of attribute types with which to build a content model. These attribute types will hopefully cover the majority of use cases, and they likely have evolved over successive versions of the CMS to cover more and more patterns.

The quantity and applicability of these attribute types varies, and this contributes greatly to the success of a CMS in its effort to accurately represent your content model.

Some common examples of attribute types available in many CMSs:

- A single-line **text field**
- A multi-line **textarea**, with or without rich text editing
- A numeric value, stored to various decimal places (a concept called **precision**)
- A date, also with varying levels of precision
- A series of discrete values, specified by a checkbox or dropdown list
- A reference to another content object
- A file upload

Specific attribute types provide a clean and intuitive editorial interface.

You could just make everything a textbox and hope the editors enter all the information correctly, but that's not at all helpful.

There exists a too little-discussed concept of **editor experience** (sometimes called **author experience**). It argues you should cater to your editors' experience *just as much as your users*. The implied benefit is a better editorial experience will directly result in better content and indirectly results in lower training and support costs.

> In my experience, the number one complaint of organizations looking to replace their current CMS is, simply, "Our editors hate it."

common

Checkbox	Date	Date/Time	Decimal
Email address	Label	Numeric	Slider
Tags	Textarea	Textbox	

A variety of built-in attribute types available when defining content types in Umbraco.

To improve editor experience, systems will offer a variety of attribute types in order to:

1. Assist editors in defining a value for the attribute

2. **Coerce values** by disallowing anything outside of the required format

Note the use of "coerce" rather than "enforce." A validation rule (discussed later) *enforces* valid entries by actively rejecting an invalid entry. A custom attribute *coerces* valid entries by making it impossible to enter anything *other* than a valid value.

A CMS usually offers some base-level customizations or settings, common to all attribute types. The most obvious are name and label – the same attribute type added multiple times to the same content type must have different names, depending on what concept it's meant to represent.

> Remember the "name" is the internal, machine representation of an attribute, and must be unique. "Label" is what's displayed to editors. Could two attributes have different names, but the same label? In most cases, this is allowed, but would be pointlessly confusing.

For example, if you're storing a simple list of employees, you might have three attributes: First Name, Last Name, and Job Title. All three of these are of an attribute type called, perhaps, "Single Line Text." This renders as a simple textbox, giving us three textboxes in which to enter our information. The attribute types are the same; they differ solely in the most basic customization: name and label.

Other universal aspects of an attribute which might be customizable are:

- Whether or not a value is required (this is technically a validation rule, discussed in a later chapter, but it's so common that it often appears as a setting)

- Whether or not the attribute has an editorial element at all (see the next section)

- Whether or not the attribute allows multiple values (discussed in a later chapter)

- Whether or not the value is searchable by default

- Whether or not the attribute is localized, and therefore has a different value for each language

- In which area of the interface the editorial element should appear (tab, group, or pane), for interfaces that can be so arranged

In some systems, these settings are universal to all attribute types, and each type might also have its own settings and rules. For example, while the concept of a value being required is applicable to both a textbox and a dropdown element, the textbox might have an additional, type-specific setting of a maximum length, which wouldn't apply to a dropdown element.

Finally, attributes assigned to a content type are always assigned in a specific order, which can be adjusted via drag-and-drop or "move up" and "move down" options. The order of attributes is critical for editorial experience and will be discussed in a later chapter.

One other thing to note – each attribute usually has an associated editorial element, but that doesn't mean a one-to-one relationship with *actual input fields*. An attribute might store some type of **compound value** formed using multiple inputs. For example, see the WordPress image earlier in this chapter – the Published Date is formed using a dropdown and four additional text fields.

The translation from a possibly complex array of input elements into a simple value that can be stored is handled by serialization code inherent to the attribute type (we'll discuss this quite a bit in the next chapter).

Also, an attribute might have *no* editorial element, for attributes not intended to be edited by humans using the interface. In some cases, an attribute might exist to store a value provided by some other process, either at the time of saving, or sometime in the future. In fact, there might be attribute values that change behind the scenes all the time, independent of when an editor actually works with the content in the interface.

For example, a Product might have an attribute for Remaining Stock, to represent how many items of this product are available to be sold. This might be updated by the inventory management system once an hour, without any human intervention. Your template developers might put a "Very few left!" banner on any product page with a Remaining Stock value of less than five. Additionally, the same update job might unpublish any product when its Remaining Stock value reaches zero. In a sense, your inventory management system is a robotic editor, occasionally changing content without human intervention.

The Remaining Stock attribute should not be editable by humans – or even viewable in the editing interface – but it is available to be read by templates and other processes.

Attribute types are the most important way to keep your content model valid and resilient – if you force a "Number" attribute, you can be reasonably sure that what goes into and out of that field is numeric. Each attribute is a single point of interaction between you editors and your model, and the type of the attribute defines the basic rules around that interaction.

Evaluation Questions

- What built-in attribute types are available?
- What universal settings are available for all attributes?

Timeout

How Content Is Stored

This chapter gets a little technical, but it provides some insight into how content moves into and out of its data store. Even if you have no development experience, push through it because it will provide valuable context later on.

Under the covers, the actual data stored in our repository is usually just one of three types:

1. A text string (a series of characters)

2. A number

3. A date

4. A block of bytes (a binary large object, or **BLOB**)

These three things are **primitive datatypes**. (That's highly differentiated term, depending on the programming language, but it fits our general usage here.)

A "string" is a series of characters in a specific order. When individual characters are "strung together," they form text. This "string of characters" differentiates it from a single character, which is usually a different datatype entirely.

Almost every attribute type will convert their *logical* value into one of those primitive values before storing it. This happens because we don't create a custom database schema for every possible attribute type – they all have to make do with a general schema, so their values have to be converted to a store-able form.

This is a fundamental theme of CMS in general – we're storing highly custom data in a generalized system. If we created a custom storage system for everything then we wouldn't need a CMS. Indeed, our desire *not* to do this is why we have CMSs in the first place.

A CMS is, in many ways, just a customization or an extension to an underlying datastore. Every CMS is backed by some datastore – usually a relational database. Any database will store information. What makes a *content management system* are the services it provides over and above simple storage.

The concept of converting a more complex data structure to a simpler one for storage is called *serialization*, while the process of restoring the complex structure from the simpler value is *deserialization*.

For example, if we need to edit and store a set of map coordinates, we will likely give our editors a visual map interface from which to pick a location. When they do, the CMS will serialize that logical value – the set of coordinates, and perhaps the zoom level the editor was at when they picked it – into something simpler. The *actual value* stored in the database is just a string of structured text, like this (XML, in this example):

```
<coordinates lat="43.55" long="-96.7" zoom="1.5"/>
```

Next time the editorial interface for this attribute needs to render and populate with the stored value, the CMS deserializes that XML back into the logical location value, and uses it to position the map in the editing interface.

> What about search? How does a serialized value like our example get searched, if, say, someone wanted to find all locations in a specific area?
>
> In most cases, serialized data can't be searched as it's written because a search engine can't "reach into" the field efficiently. To enable searching, the data is often written into a search index in an entirely different format.
>
> We'll talk about supplemental indexing in a later chapter.

The point of this chapter is that many attribute types are just fancy editorial elements to arrive at one of the primitive datatypes that can be stored.

Another example: a CMS might offer a "Number" attribute type, into which an editor can enter a number. It might also offer a "Slider" field which lets the edit drag a slider to the right or left to increase or decrease a numeric value. *Both of these attributes are storing primitive numbers*, they only differ in the interface they offer editors to express the desired value.

> So why use numbers and dates? Everything can be stored as text, so why not just do that? Sorting, mainly. Text, numbers, and dates are sorted differently (a concept known as **collation**), so storing them as their native types allows them to be sorted efficiently.

To re-state the note from the beginning of the chapter, this information certainly isn't necessary to work with a content model or a CMS. In fact, CMSs go to great lengths to hide all of this from you. A CMS works very hard to make storing content seem like magic, and not exposing you to all the gory details of how it gets done.

Evaluation Criteria #4

How is content represented in the API?

We've talked about types and attributes as an editorial feature – they provide an optimized editorial interface, and they assist editors in ensuring the correct value is stored. So far, this has been about *writing* content.

However, what about the other side? How can types and attributes help when *reading* content? When integration or template developers need to retrieve a content object to work with it, what data construct do they actually get back from the repository?

First, a programming primer.

Most programming languages today are **object oriented** ("object oriented programming" is somewhat hilariously abbreviated as "OOP"). This style of programming means units of code logic are defined in structures called "classes," from which you can create "objects." Objects expose data in "properties" and can perform actions called "methods."

The benefit of OOP is you can work with an object – tell it to do things and ask it for information – without having to know what it's doing inside to get any of the work done.

For example, you might have an object called "War and Peace" which is created from the `Book` class. You can ask "War and Peace" for its `Title` or tell it to do something like `TurnThePage` and expect responses from it, but you have no idea how it's doing any of this. The actual code to do this is internal to the Book class.

The external structures that are exposed to you – the `Title` property or the `TurnThePage` method – are known as the **interface**. The code inside of the class that actually performs the required processing is known as the **implementation**. A key benefit of OOP is you don't have to concern yourself with the implementation, so long as you know what to expect when you invoke different aspects of the interface.

When you press the button on the remote control to turn on your TV, you have no idea about the wires, electrons, and light pulses invoked to make the TV light up. That's the *implementation*. The button you press is the *interface*, and so long as the TV lights up, that's all you need to know.

A technician could sneak in while you were away and completely change the innards of how the remote control works, but so long as the TV still lights up when you press the button, you would neither know nor care. The button interface completely abstracts you away from the technical implementation of turning on the TV.

This is generally considered a clean and helpful way to manage code. If I have a `Book` object anywhere in my codebase, I can trust it will have the same interface, without me having to scatter or duplicate code everywhere. If I want to change how it does something, I can change the implementation inside the class and trust that change will be reflected everywhere it's used.

The parallels to content management should be very clear –

- A content type is a Class
- A content object is an Object
- An attribute is a Property

Thus, it's *very* helpful if content objects can be automatically translated into code objects when they're retrieved. In your programming code, you can have a `Book` class with a property for `Title` and know it will automatically retrieve the correct attribute value.

This is called **strong typing**, which means there's a parallel between the content type and a class in the programming language, and the CMS will handle the translation automatically.

Some systems don't strongly type content objects, and they are all represented as a generic, catch-all class – so-called **weak typing** – when developers need to work with them.

Instead of `Book`, the class might be called something like `ContentObject` or `Item`. Instead of reading named properties on the object like `Title`, there is some generic method for accessing attributes, like `GetAttribute("Title")`.

This is not a major problem, it just means more work for the developer, and a slightly increased chance of error if there's an invalid attribute value.

Strong-typing isn't just for objects. Attribute values can be strongly-typed as well.

In the last chapter, we discussed how an attribute's logical value is serialized into a primitive value for storage. The resulting primitive value – the string of XML in the example – is easy to store in a generalized datastore, but it isn't ideal for developers. They'd rather get that in some native programming construct of whatever language they're working in.

Depending on the system, the value stored in the attribute might be accessible as a strongly typed object, meaning it's accessed as a true representation of the data stored in it, in whatever programming or templating language the CMS uses.

To take the map example, you might deserialize that back into a helpful object value for your template developers to use (JavaScript/JSON, in this example):

```
{ latitude: 43.55, longitude: -96.7, zoom: 1.5 }
```

This allows the deserialization to be consistent, so not everyone needing to work with the data is creating their own method to make sense of the primitive value. This clearly makes life easier for the developers charged with integrating and templating the system.

In addition to simply reading data values, it's sometimes helpful to have other code logic available from a class to make the underlying content object easier to work with.

For example, let's say you have a Chapter with an attribute for Title. There's also an attribute called Header, to represent a shortened title to print at the top of each page of that chapter. In most cases, the Header will be explicitly entered as a shorter version of Title. However, in some cases, Title is already short enough, so you just want to use it instead of entering an explicit Header.

> This is literally the content model used for this guide. When printed, the header at the top of the right-hand pages are shorter versions of the chapter titles, using the exact logic described above. The titles of some chapters are short enough that the header doesn't need to be explicitly specified.

This is simple enough to code in almost any programming language. Here it is as a class property in C#:

```
HeaderDisplay => Header ?? Title;
```

The ?? operator is called a "null coalesce," and says, "if there's nothing in the value to the left of me, return what's to the right of me instead."

In this example, HeaderDisplay becomes a pseudo-attribute with no actual, entered value of its own. Instead, it performs some logical processing to return the value of Header if that's defined, and Title if it's not.

Note *this has nothing to do with the CMS*. Everything above is in C#, which is an underlying programming language. The CMS has no idea this is being done, but this functionality is enabled by the CMS's ability to automatically deserialize a Chapter content object into a `Chapter` class in C#, onto which we can add helpful code.

If you can't do this, then the functional goal above is still possible, your developers just have to write this code in other ways, and for each context. For example, your template developer might have to write a special template function in whatever templating language they're using. And your back-end developer might have to duplicate the above logic in some other method that's accessible to their code.

This chapter was a bit of a stretch from the core discussion of content modeling, but it matters because a strongly-typed API enables you to perform pseudo-modeling operations in your code.

The concept of "failing over" from Header to Title is logic that belongs to Chapter, and if you have access to the full array of features in your underlying language, you can keep this logic clean and centralized. We have essentially created a new attribute – HeaderDisplay – in code, rather than as actual content. The final, effective value originates in *logic*, not *data*.

This goes back to the core principle of maintainability – not so much of your specific content model, but of the underlying code in particular, and the entire integration effort in general.

Evaluation Questions

- When retrieving content for integration or templating, what data structure is a content object represented as in code?
- How can calculated attributes or other helper code be represented on objects for usage in templating or integration?

Evaluation Criteria #5

How can attribute values be validated?

Attribute types use the editorial interface to coerce editors into creating valid attribute values. Our mapping example from the last chapter would offer editors nothing but a map from which they could pick a location, into which we would extract the coordinates. Thankfully, there's no way an editor could type the entire text of *War and Peace* into that editorial element.

Value coercion is the first line of content modeling resiliency.

But sometimes you can't rely only on coercion because the format of the value needs additional evaluation for logical truth. Therefore, our fallback position is validation rules.

A validation rule is a "test" to ensure a proposed value logically satisfies some condition. Failure to pass the test results in an error and a refusal of the system to store the value, which usually manifests as a refusal to store the entire set of changes of which the invalid value is a part.

As the father of teenagers, the idiom I hate most in the world is: "Rules were made to be broken."

No they were not. This is literally the exact opposite reason rules are created.

The most basic validation is that a value exists at all – whether or not it is **required**.

If I'm writing an Article, it might have a Date Published, and this has to exist before the article is considered publishable. If an article existed without a Date Published, several undesirable things might happen – the article might sort oddly, or not at all; or there would be a big blank space in the templated output.

Most systems will allow you to require a value for a particular attribute. When this is enforced, the content cannot be saved until a value is provided.

An example of multiple missing attributes preventing an object from being saved in Drupal.

As discussed above, this validation usually applies to this *entire* set of changes – there could be 100 other attributes, and saving the entire thing will be prevented by a single missing attribute value.

This can be frustrating for editors, because they might not have the value for some particular reason (for example, if they're collaborating with someone else on the content), so an editor will often put a placeholder value so the content can be saved, with the intention of fixing it later.

The Editorial Lifecycle

Content in a CMS goes through an **editorial lifecycle** where a specific version of a content object passes through several states. This is different for every system, but the following are common.

1. When content is loaded into an editorial interface, it is considered **checked**

out to a particular editor. Other editors might see that the content is locked and cannot be edited.

2. When an editor has made their changes and submitted them, content is **saved** back to the repository, which means it is stored, *but not checked in*. The current editor still has a lock on it. (Perhaps the editor just needed to go get lunch. Or worse, perhaps they went on vacation.)

3. Content is **checked in** when the current editor is done working with it, and releases the lock on it. Checking content in necessarily involves saving changes as well. The content can now be checked out by someone else.

4. Content is **submitted** when an editor begins the process of publishing the content. The process might be direct, or it might be a series of reviews and approvals which have to pass satisfactorily.

5. Content is **published** when editing and approvals are complete, and the content can be displayed to its intended audience. If the content needs to be edited again, the cycle starts anew, but *with a new version of the content*. So, Version #1 remains published, and Version #2 is created and checked-out, and we go back to Step 1.

The specifics differ between systems, but the lifecycle described above is relatively common. In most systems, validation occurs whenever an editor attempts to save content back to the repository (step #2).

A required field cannot be stored without a value, but there's a more subtle issue here about what "no value" means.

In general programming, there's some surprisingly deep theory behind the concept of a **null value**. A null literally means "nothing," as opposed to what we might normally consider nothing.

- For text, humans would usually consider empty text to be no value but your system might not. A text string of zero characters might still be considered a value. To a computer, this still a string of text, it just has no characters. This is entirely different than a number or a date.

- For a number, we often consider zero to be no value but it's not. Zero only means no value when referring to specific instance of a range – zero ice cream cones certainly means no ice cream cones, but *zero is still a value*.

- For a date...can we have no date? If we talk about a "date," then it's tough to say there's nothing there. In fact, many systems have a completely separate datatype for "nullable date." When a date is required but not provided, many languages have a default date – for example, Unix-based systems will default a missing date to December 31, 1969.

A lot of this discussion depends on the underling programming framework. Different languages are more or less forgiving of missing values.

From a processing standpoint, if there's a default value, you just need to know what it is so you can compare. If you know the default date is "1969-12-31" and that date in unlikely to mean anything in your scenario, you can just compare against that to determine if a value is missing.

Beyond requiring a value, we often want to ensure some **logical validity** to the content, meaning a value that has some meaning when taken in the context of what the attribute is meant to represent.

Sure, something might be a number at its most basic level, but is it the *right kind* of number? If we're compiling a list of movies and we want an attribute to store the year of release, then what do we actually want? We can ask for a number, but "1,976,566.539" is a number, yet that's clearly *way* outside of the bounds of what we're looking for.

However, if we were storing the Gross Domestic Product of a small nation, then perhaps "1,976,566.539" is quite valid.

It could be said that we want a four-digit number – certainly no movies were created before 1000AD, and 10000AD is a long way away. But if we want to get stricter, we could say we want a number between 1878 and...today? Or do you want to also count movies released in the next few years? So, 2025, to be safe?

The larger point here is that primitive datatype validation is not enough. We want to validate the *logical concept* of what the attribute value is intended to represent.

Some common validation rule types:

- **Range**, for those values that exist on a scale, meaning the value is between two values, or greater or less than a single value
- **Pattern**, for text values that need to be in a particular format (dates must be "yyyy-mm-dd", for example); these are usually regular expressions (see below)
- Length, for text, in both directions (usually to enforce a maximum, but sometimes a minimum)

And there are likely more specific validation rules for more specific attribute types offered by different systems.

Validation rules often overlap, especially when **regular expression (regex)** pattern matching is available.

Regular expressions are a concept in computing where a text value can be interrogated for conformance to a defined pattern. You can require the existence of specific types of characters, in a specific order.

> When I first encountered the term "regular expression," it seemed odd to me. A "regular language" in computing is just a language that conforms to rules – "regular" being a form of "regulate." So, the term regular expression can be interpreted as "the expression of a set of rules," which makes sense.
>
> The concept of regular languages or grammars goes all the way back to a seminal 1956 paper[1] on written (non-computing) language construction by Noam Chomsky.

Some examples of simple regular expressions:

- To ensure text is between 5 and 10 characters, you might have a regex pattern of `[\S]{5,10}`. That says, "a non-whitespace character at least five times, but not more than 10."

- Required text can be represented as `[\S]+`. That says, "a non-whitespace character any number of times more that zero."

- A four-digit year can be `[0-9]{4}`. That says, "a numeric digit exactly four times."

What's handy is that pattern validation can identify and validate custom patterns the CMS can't know about beforehand.

For example, if you need an editor to enter a product number, and the format of your product number is three upper-case letters, a dash, four numeric digits, another dash, and one more digit (ex. "GTF-6395-2"), that's easily validated against the pattern:

- `^[A-Z]{3}-[0-9]{4}-[0-9]$`

Anything not matching that pattern would fail validation.

Regular expressions don't "understand" the content other than just as an arbitrary list of characters. Sure, it can make sure something is a string of four nu-

---

1. *The Wikipedia page on The Chomsky Hierarchy. https://en.wikipedia.org/wiki/Chomsky_hierarchy*

meric digits, but it doesn't "know" that's a number, much less that it's supposed to represent a year.

Regex just understands patterns. It doesn't care what those patterns mean.

Item name filter

All or part of the item name:

r(?=e)   Clear Filter

Use: Regular Expression ▾

An example setting up a regular expression pattern validation in Sitecore.

As discussed above, validation normally occurs whenever an editor attempts to save content back to the repository, either new content that didn't exist, or existing content that has been changed. What this means is content cannot leave the editorial interface until it passes all validation rules.

Remember that "save" is not the same as "publish." A particular version of content will likely be saved multiple times, then published once. An editor might work on a blog post over the course of a week, for example. The editor will change the content, save it, change it again, save it, and over and over before finally publishing the result.

To relieve the "validation pressure," some systems can **delay validation**. Either they run validation rules only before content is *published*, or different rules can be configured to execute at different phases of the editorial lifecycle – some at save, some at check-in, some at publish, etc.

Loosening the timing of validation rules can make life easier for editors. Sometimes it's helpful to allow looser rules during content development so editors can "rough in" content without any requirement to pass all validation. As long as content validation checks happen prior to publish, then there's no risk invalid content will be exposed to the public.

Note that in many systems, the built-in attribute of Name is absolutely non-negotiable. If content doesn't have a name, many parts of the editorial UI might be unusable, so this is always required before content can even be created.

If validation is delayed, missing values need to be checked for and handled if that content is processed.

If an editor wanted to preview her blog post, for example, the template would need to be coded to handle a situation where the incomplete blog post might not have a subtitle. In this case, the template could either just skip that section completely, or render some placeholder text ("Subtitle Goes Here").

Prismic is a headless CMS that went a step further: *they abolished the idea of required fields altogether*, and defended this philosophy in a blog post[1]. Their argument was that requiring data makes for a poor editorial experience, and templates should just account for potentially invalid content. It's a controversial position.

Some systems will allow the assignment of **default values** to attributes.

If an Article needs a Date Published value, then the system might enter the current date as the default value when an editor is creating a new content object of that type. Normally, we wouldn't consider this validation, but there's a slight twist to default values that blurs the boundary a bit.

Default values can operate on two models:

1. A default value can simply pre-fill the editorial element to provide a value on new object creation, which is just a usability feature for editors. If a particular value is common (example: the current date as the Date Published for a blog post), then providing a default saves some keystrokes and provides some suggestive value. An editor can always change the default value if desired.

2. Alternately, a default value can be added prior to save *only when nothing is entered for an attribute*. So, if an attribute value is required, the interface might not enforce that and allow the editor to press the "Save" button without value, but the default value will be added before the content is *actually* saved.

That latter feature is just validation in another form. It's making an attribute required, but using logical processing to fill in the value when it's not provided.

There are some usability concerns here, since it can confuse editors if they're actually trying to indicate no value but the content continues to be published

---

1. *"Unpopular opinion: why required fields lead to terrible UX". https://prismic.io/blog/required-fields*

with a value added. However, this would be either (1) a training issue, or (2) a documentation issue, since this should be noted in some help text somewhere in the interface.

The "forced default value" feature can also be enforced with API-level programming against an event model. Many systems will provide a "Content Saving" or "Before Content Save" event, in which values can be modified (and a default value is added) before storage.

Attributes should be expected to support multiple validation rules.

This seems straightforward, but if an attribute is governed by more than one rule:

- Do they execute in a particular order?
- Does one rule failure prevent the others from executing? (If so, then they would logically *have* to be in a specified order.)
- Does a particular rule only execute under specific circumstances?

For example, if a value is required, *and* forced to conform to a particular pattern or range, is the latter rule dependent on the former?

This takes us back to our prior discussion of what "no value" means – if a numeric value is required to be between 5 and 10, and the editor enters nothing, which rule is it failing? That nothing was entered at all, or that we assumed nothing meant "0" and that's out of range? That distinction seems academic, but a lot of systems would display both error messages in that situation.

Two error messages might just be annoying, but what if you didn't want to require a value? So your validation logic is: *only if a value is entered*, it must be between 5 and 10. This means the value is no longer required, and no value should pass validation.

Some systems have provisions for **conditional validation** which will apply some logic to validation. For example, a rule might only run if a value was entered – no value is considered valid and requires no further validation. Or, the rules might run in series, with the first failure short-circuiting all the rules following it.

This logic can get tricky, and it's likely the rules for these situations are baked into the system. When you run into limits here, you'll often have to resort to custom validation.

Enforcing attribute validation is a key step in making a content model resilient. It prevents editors from making mistakes which cause more serious errors and confusion later in the publishing pipeline.

Additionally, it helps the CMS understand the content model and provide more contextual help when editors are trying to create content. An error isn't universally undesirable – many times, it's a key component in training editors and assisting in their discovery of the system and the content model.

Now let's talk about how a CMS can use the developing model to assist editors further.

Evaluation Questions

- What validation rules are globally available for all attribute types?
- Can attribute values be required?
- Can text-based attributes be validated by regular expressions or other pattern matching?
- When is attribute validation executed – only on save, or can different validation rules be assigned to different points in the editorial lifecycle?
- How are multiple triggered validation rules represented to editors, and can the execution of rules be conditional on the status of other rules?
- Can default values be assigned to attributes, and are these merely pre-entered in the interface, or are they assigned when no other value is provided?

Evaluation Criteria #6

How is the model supported in the editorial interface?

We've been dancing in and around a principle for all the prior chapters, but let's state it for the record: a key benefit of a well-conceived content model implemented in a competent CMS is an improved editorial interface.

The editorial interface of a CMS is not custom, it's **derived** – meaning the CMS examines the defined content model and algorithmically determines how it should be displayed and behave.

And this is a great thing. In fact, the avoidance of writing custom interfaces for every content type is a key benefit of using a CMS in the first place. You can describe your content in logical terms, and your CMS should automatically generate a functional interface for your editors.

The only way the CMS knows how to display the editorial interface, however, is because of how the content model is defined, which goes back to the core value of descriptiveness. The descriptive value of the model and how it's interpreted by the CMS contributes to how well the editorial interface will function.

The most basic aspect of the editorial interface might be labeling the editorial element of each attribute. Every CMS lets you name an attribute for internal reference, and most allow you to give each attribute a clearer, more human-readable label to display to editors.

Also helpful is the ability to provide explanatory text that's available from the interface, to give editors extra information on how each editorial element works, and how each attribute contributes to the object it forms.

Helper text under attribute labels in Episerver.

Editors don't like to get stuck, and there's little more infuriating than staring down a page full of poorly labeled, cryptic input fields with no idea what each one does. If you can't provide at least the most basic description to your editors, not much else matters in terms of usability.

Based on the attribute type, the CMS will display a different editorial element designed to help an editor create or modify a value for it.

Some common interface elements are:

- Rich text editors to generate HTML (it's very common to have a "text" attribute, and a "rich text" attribute, to differentiate them). Also becoming more common is a **Markdown** editor, often with tabbed or split-screen preview

- Date pickers that let editors scroll through a calendar (note these are often *less* usable than simple, validated text entry, so it's handy to be able to use both – pick a date if you want, but enter it by keystroke if that's easier)

- Numeric fields which only accept numbers and occasionally provide "increment" and "decrement" buttons (the utility of which is highly questionable)

- Masked fields which provide interstitial punctuation based on format – for instance, a text field that automatically places decimals and commas in dollar amounts, or a phone number field that adds dashes in the correct locations (which is, admittedly, culturally specific)

- Selection ("dropdown") fields which limit a choice to a specific set of values

- Content browsing and search tools that allow the selection of other content objects (these are used for referential attributes, which we'll discuss in a later chapter).

- File upload tools

Editorial element selection is the first line of editorial usability.

An example of an editorial element for a linked image in Cloud CMS. The element offers three data points: (1) the image to use, (2) the desired ALT text, and (3) the content to which it should be linked. The editor is designed to assist editors in creating and editing valid data, and minimize the chance they'll provide an invalid entry.

The editorial interface is where content modeling intersects with **editorial usability**. While the quality of the editorial interface isn't a direct feature of the content model, our ability to affect the editorial interface will often impact how you put your content model together. A well-thought out set of editorial tools can make you more confident that editors will be able to safely generate quality content.

It's not at all uncommon to design a content model for maximum editorial usability, rather than to be exactly what's needed to describe the content. Occasionally, the right answer is to make concessions and modifications to the model to decrease chances for human confusion. Many confused editors can trace their problems to a content designer trying to be too clever.

The ability to order and group the editorial interface is also helpful.

Attributes should be presented to editors in a logical sequence, usually by perceived importance to the content (Title first, for example), and with priority to required fields. While it's not necessary to have all required attributes first, it's probably good practice to keep them somewhere near the top of the interface.

Some systems will allow you to arrange attributes into tabs, collapsing sections, or other pseudo-paged groupings. Attributes common to a particular use case can be kept together, and labeled to make their usage and relationship clear to editors. For example, the attributes for META tags (Keywords, Description, etc.) might be grouped together under a tab for "SEO."

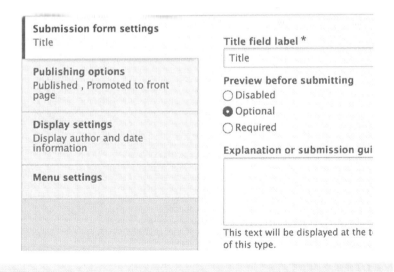

An example of attributes grouped into tabs in Drupal.

Clear error messages are important.

Validation rules should be able to return messages specific to the validation issue, rather than something generic, and these messages should be visually associated with the invalid attribute. In the event the invalid attribute is buried below the fold, there should be some clear visual notification that an error is lurking somewhere outside the viewing area.

Oftentimes, it's helpful to suppress attribute editing from the interface, by either removing attributes altogether, or preventing them from being edited.

Then why have them? Why not just remove the attribute from the model? Because sometimes that's not an option, and sometimes we still want the attribute, we just don't want a human to change the value.

We discussed non-editable properties in a prior chapter (the hidden Remaining Stock attribute). Updating attributes using the API is quite common, and it would be rare for attributes updated this way to *also* allow direct editorial input.

Sometimes, however, we want to remove built-in attributes from the interface when they're not being used, to prevent confusion for editors who might think they have a purpose. Built-in attributes can't actually be removed from the model, but they can sometimes be hidden.

In one particular CMS, for example, we never used the default categorization system, even though a category selection attribute was part of the built-in model and was prominent in every editing interface. The first thing we did in every implementation was remove this attribute from the editorial interface.

In another situation, we had First Name and Last Name attributes, but the requirements dictated that the Name of the content object should always be "Last Name, First Name" – a **calculated attribute value**. We were able to hide the Name attribute, suppress the required validation, then use event programming to set it to the correct value using the values from First Name and Last Name attributes before saving it.

Beyond just the actual interface to edit content, a system needs to support the finding of content based on the defined model.

Many systems will allow editors to search and filter for content by type. In tree-based systems (discussed later), it's common to be able to navigate content by spatial location – open "branches" of the tree to display the children of a particular content object.

Additionally, when heterogeneous content is listed in any form, it's very helpful to see some indicator of the content type. Some systems provide visual markers or indicators – when displayed in a tree or a list, for example, each content object might display an icon to indicate its type.

> The effect icons have on recall and retention should not be underestimated. I've worked with systems that allowed custom iconography and systems that did not. The difference in editorial usability, understanding, and comfort is remarkable.

Clearly, this chapter has crossed over some lines into disciplines not specifically about content modeling. But other disciplines intersect, and editorial usability is one of them.

Attribute types and validation rules are fundamentally concerned with content model resiliency – protecting the logical integrity of our content model by preventing the entry of invalid data.

Editorial usability has the same effect. Editors are not purposefully trying to enter invalid content. Rather it happens because the interface they had to work with was confusing and allowed them to do it without being challenged.

Evaluation Questions

- Do attributes have a human-friendly label to display to editors?
- Can longer-form help text be made available in the interface for each attribute?
- Can the order that attributes are displayed in the interface be controlled?
- Can attributes be grouped into panes, tabs, or sections?
- How are validation error messages displayed to editors?
- Can unnecessary built-in attributes be suppressed from the UI altogether?
- Does the editorial UI allow custom iconography to represent concepts like content types?

Can an attribute value be a reference to another object?

So far, we've explained **discrete content modeling**, which is the modeling of a self-contained object.

We've dealt with attributes like Title and Body with the implicit assumption these are all unique to a single object and contained wholly within it. Content Object #1 has a Title and Content Object #2 as a Title and these two things have no relationship to each other. Each content object is a container for its own content, and nothing extends past the edges of that container.

> Don't confuse "discreet" with "discrete." The former means private or secret. The latter is often used in programming, and it means "constituting a separate thing consisting of unconnected distinct parts."

Sometimes, however, it's helpful for a content object to have a relationship with another object. We need to create a link between the two at the attribute level.

This is the opposite of discrete content modeling – this is **relational content modeling** – the modeling of relationships between content objects.

Say you have an Article type which stores some information about the author – there are attributes for Author First Name, Author Last Name, and Author Email.

You start to realize, however, you're duplicating a lot of information. Bob has written 300 articles, and his information is embedded on all of them, and he just changed his email address.

Additionally, let's say you'd like Bob to have his own page, where you can display some extra information about him and provide a list of his articles. However, Bob isn't an actual content object. Remember, Bob's representation in content only exists as a handful of attributes, duplicated on hundreds of other objects.

What you need to do is create a content object to represent Bob, then somehow link all those 300 articles to that single object in such a way that Bob's object knows about all 300 articles, and all 300 articles know about Bob's object.

You need to create a new type for Author. You can create attributes like First Name, Last Name, and Email. In doing this, you can create a content object for Bob (and for every other author), and give him his own page.

Then, you need to link Bob and his articles together. Ideally, we can do this with a **referential attribute**, which is an attribute value that doesn't hold any actual data, but is just a reference to another object. The Author attribute on Article now links over to Bob's Author object. When you're rendering our Article, you just display Bob's name and email from whatever is on the linked Author object *at that moment*.

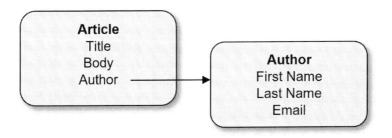

In this model, Author doesn't hold any data other than a reference to an Author object somewhere else in the repository.

This model realizes some efficiencies and benefits by the association. Every article now "knows" the object of the author who wrote it, and you can maintain this person's information in one place. With the usage of referential attributes, our repository of content begins to become a network or a **graph** of connections.

Ideally, all prior functionality works the same with referential attributes.

- All validation rules are still available

- We can still create custom validation, if we need to (see)

- If repeating attributes are offered (see), they also apply to referential attributes (an article might have multiple authors, for example)

The complicating factor of referential modeling is that once we have a link between two content objects, we open a Pandora's Box of potential issues. Remember the 300 articles linked to Bob? Well, Bob just quit in spectacular fashion and management wants him off the website.

Okay, just delete him.

Wait... Since that attribute is a reference, the system will automatically delete all the references to Bob's object when that object is deleted. That will leave 300 content objects with an empty Author attribute

Is this a problem? Maybe not. It could be Author was optional anyway – let's say some articles didn't have one, and the template is designed to work around an empty attribute without breaking.

What if they *were* required? What if the template needs a populated Author attribute or else it breaks along with a dozen integrations to external systems, all of them expecting a populated Author attribute (this goes back to our discussion of "predictability" in).

Maintaining rules around content references is the concept of **referential integrity** or **dependency management**. Literally, how do you maintain the integrity of your references?

In some systems, you'll be prevented from deleting an object if there are inbound references from other objects. Other systems will prompt you to mass-replace the reference with a reference to another object. Others will just allow you to complete the deletion and nullify all the references.

Breaking Links

☐ ✕

Other items contain links to this item or its subitems. These links should be updated to prevent broken links.

Action

◉ Remove links

◯ Link to another item

◯ Leave links – the links will appear in the Broken Links report

Edit Links

When attempting to delete an object with inbound links, Sitecore offers multiple options to remove, repair, or ignore the link you're about to break.

Additionally, many systems will offer a proactive interface editors can access to show them links between this item and others, separate from the warnings given prior to deletion.

Beyond referential attributes, a system should also extract references from rich text. If an anchor tag inside HTML somewhere in an attribute on Object A links to a URL associated with Object B, this should be discovered and enforced in the same way as a referential attribute.

Another consideration is **reference directedness**, which describes the directionality of the link – are links inbound, outbound, or both?

In our prior example, an article clearly points at Bob's Author content object, but is the inverse true? When examining Bob's Author object, can you follow 300 inbound links back to the corresponding Article object? If so, then the links are considered **bi-directional**; if not, then they're are **unidirectional**.

Social media provides a handy illustration –

On Facebook, if we become "friends," this is reciprocal. If I am your friend, then you are mine as well. It's the same way with "connections" on LinkedIn. These are bi-directional links.

Conversely, Twitter and Instagram have the concept of "followers." I can follow you, but you don't have to follow me back. The concept of me following you and you following me are two separate things. These links are uni-directional.

> If we were to follow each other, we would actually create two separate one-way links.

Bi-directional references are unfortunately uncommon in CMS. What makes it difficult is there's no "receiving" attribute on the Author object.

If you have Bob's object in hand, what do you check to find the inbound links? Logic would say there should be an Articles attribute which contains 300 references, but this would involve the CMS adding a "pseudo-attribute" on a type (or multiple types, if any type can be linked to), and this isn't functionality you'll find often.

What you can usually do is just search from the other direction: find Article objects that include a reference to Bob's object in their Author attribute. It's not quite as elegant or intuitive, but it provides the same basic result.

When editors are working with a referential property, the editorial interface matters. A referential attribute has to provide an easy way to find another specific object, potentially from *thousands* of other objects.

With a limited number of objects, a simple dropdown may work. Some systems have the "two-pane" approach where you can scroll through options in the left pane, and press a button to move them to the right pane.

Other systems allow browsing or searching, or some combination of the two, depending on the underlying structure of the content in the system. In tree-based systems, you can usually browse through the tree for another object. Other systems have a search interface which allows some form of full-text searching.

These interfaces usually pop up in model dialogs positioned over the rest of the editorial interface. (How did we do this before modals were possible? *Very poorly*.)

A content object selector modal in Episerver. This overlays the editing interface (faded, in the background, to the left of the modal), and allows the editor to select a linked content object. In this case, all types are allowed. However, referential attributes in Episerver can be limited by type, and invalid types would be displayed in a shade of gray and would not be selectable.

Object selection may or may not respect permissions. If an editor doesn't have permission to view a certain content object, should they be able to select it as a link? Usually not, since, in most systems, permissions also apply to editors and would therefore restrict content even in the editorial interface.

And what if there's a permissions mismatch – what if our Article object had much looser permissions than our Author object, so a viewer might be able to view the article but not the author? If the system is managing permissions correctly, this might cause a problem when trying to view the content.

We can account for this in the rendering template, but it might be helpful if the editor was warned in advance that the permissions of the objects don't match.

Referential attributes should be type-limited, which hopefully filters what objects can be selected.

In our example, we clearly should only allow the Author attribute to link to Author objects. In some cases you might not have any restrictions – for example, something like Related Content could be *any* type. But using a referential attribute usually means you're piecing together a network of objects, and they'll usually always be based on type.

Less ideal would be if any object can be selected, but type *validation* still occurs. So, the editor could select any object, but when a save was attempted, the attribute would fail validation. This would prevent invalid content, but usability is poor because then the editor has to go through the selection process again. If an object will fail validation for type, best not to allow its selection at all.

Using referential attributes, we can implement the loose pattern of a **composite object**, or **object assembly**. This is a content structure which carries minimal content in and of itself, and is just a collection of references to other objects which are labeled and structured in such a way to impart greater meaning.

For example, we might create a type for Committee, which we define as follows:

- Name
- Description
- Department (reference to a Department)
- Chair (reference to an Employee object)
- Vice Chair (reference to an Employee object)
- Members (repeating reference to multiple Employee objects)
- Minutes (repeating reference to multiple Document objects)
- Meeting Location (reference to a Facility object)

As you can see, our Committee object carries very little "on board" content. Rather, it's built from multiple other content objects assembled in a structure that imparts some larger meaning. A new object emerges from the aggregation of references. Our Committee type becomes a framework on which to "hang" other objects and create something larger.

This is not an explicit feature, but just a handy pattern achieved through a combination of typed, referential attributes. (The repetition aspect is handy as well, but not technically required.)

Referential attributes are powerful and can keep your content model more manageable by preventing the duplication of attribute values. However, you open a door to referential integrity issues. Once you extend the content of an object past the edges of that object, there are unintended consequences and edge cases you need to be prepared to handle.

The science of links between entities is known as **graph theory** and there's huge reservoir of research in this field. The original PageRank algorithm that powered Google was fundamentally an implementation of graph theory to rank and score links between web pages. Graph theory is used in fields as diverse as epidemiology and city planning, whenever discrete entities of any type might be somehow connected to each other and that relationship has an effect on one or both of them.

Evaluation Questions

- Can an attribute value be a reference to another object?
- How is the target object located and entered in the attribute from the interface?
- Can target objects be limited by type?
- Can referential attributes repeat?
- How do permissions affect an editor's ability to select a target object?
- If an editor attempts to delete a object which is the target or one more links, is the editor warned?
- From the interface, can editors view all objects that are linked to a specific content object?
- How are references discovered – is this limited to referential attributes, or is rich text searched for links?
- Are references uni-directional or bi-directional?
- From the API, is it possible to find all objects with an inbound link to a specific object?

Timeout

Let's Evaluate the Current Level of Functionality

We've described a fair amount of functionality. Let's take a quick timeout here to wrap up what we've detailed into a hypothetical CMS and then consider what that gets us.

Here's what we've talked about so far, and what a theoretical system encompassing all of the discussed functionality would look like:

- It would have a built-in model of some kind, perhaps consisting of a Title, Body, URL Segment, Publication Date, and Categories assignment for every content object. We'll assume this is a web-focused system, so the Body attribute would consist of rich text, and there is no distinction between content and metadata.

- This built-in model could be extended into multiple, named content types with the addition of new attribute types. Each content type could be instantiated into multiple content objects of that named type.

- We have a variety of attribute types available to be added to the built-in model to create a new content type – simple text, rich text, checkboxes, selection lists, date pickers, etc. All these types provide a custom interface element for editors to use when creating content. The interface elements all coerce the creation of an attribute value of a specific format, and they prevent editors from creating invalid values.

- The attribute values can be logically validated by a variety of rules. Values can be required, default values can be specified, and they can be tested against ranges (for numbers, dates, or text length) or regular expression patterns. Each attribute can be assigned multiple rules, and this validation can be deferred until an editor attempts to publish the content. Validation error messages can be custom to each attribute.

- Attributes can be labeled with a title to be displayed to editors. Each attribute can have helpful explanatory text, accessible from the editorial interface. Attributes can be placed in a specific order on the editorial interface, and can be arranged into logical groupings.

- Attributes can be references to other content objects. These references can be coerced by type, and a dependency management system will notify us of potentially broken references before we delete objects.

- When working with retrieved content objects, they are converted into native data structures from the underlying programming language, and we can add additional logic to those structures to support pseudo-attributes as necessary.

This is a system that incorporates every desirable feature we've discussed so far. What we've described above is a fairly competent system, and one that reflects quite a bit of what's available in the market today. Fifteen years ago, in fact, this might have been considered advanced.

If our system only included the functionality we've described so far and nothing else, it would be simplistic but serviceable, and a competent integration team could use it as a fundamentally sound tool.

It's also worth noting this: at this point, *we've essentially just duplicated the functionality of a relational database*.

- Content types are tables
- Attributes are data-typed columns
- Content objects are table rows
- Validation rules are field constraints
- Referential attributes are foreign keys

This isn't to say the work we've done so far has just gotten us back to the start, because remember that a CMS provides considerable functionality *around* content modeling. In addition to supporting a set of database-like functionality, a CMS gives you things like automatic editorial interfaces, workflow, permissions, templating, delivery, etc. It is fair to say that a CMS is a superset of database functionality – a "super database," if you will.

We still have a long way to ago, and a lot of advanced functionality to cover, but it's a fair point to say that the above functionality is the "table stakes" of competent content management at the current state of the industry.

If your system cannot support almost all of the above base functionality, then it's either behind the curve, or it's not designed to be a general-purpose CMS.

At a casino, "table stakes" represents the minimum bet you must place to enter a particular card game. If you can't meet the table stakes, you can't play.

Another term for the same thing is "seatbelt requirement." Every car has to have seatbelts, so no car commercial is going to exclaim, "Includes seatbelts!" It's just assumed that if you're selling a car, it has seatbelts. That's a base-level requirement you don't get extra points for.

And these requirements keep creeping forward. In the 70s, most cars didn't have automatic transmissions, power windows, or air conditioning. Today, it's often impossible to buy a car without those features. In every realm of technology, what was once advanced eventually becomes standard.

Evaluation Criteria #8

Can an attribute value be an embedded content object?

In the last chapter, we discussed attribute values which are references to content objects stored somewhere else in the repository. This is helpful as it means we can compose objects from multiple sources.

A key point of referential attributes is that the other object is independent – it exists somewhere else in the repository, it can be edited and deleted independently, and more than one object can link to it (remember that Bob's author object in the example was linked to by 300 different article objects).

There's another way to achieve object composition through a form of "typed attributes," meaning an attribute value that is, in itself, a wholly contained content object. This value could be called an **embedded object**.

The key is that *the entire object itself* is the attribute value, not just an object reference. A complete object is a "captive" inside an attribute. It is not independent, and it cannot be edited or deleted anywhere other than in the context of its owning object. And if the owning object is deleted, the embedded object is deleted too.

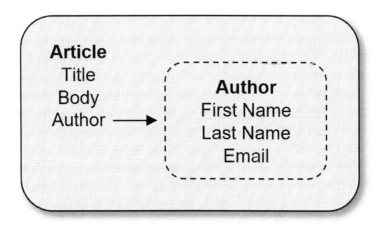

The model of typed attribute values. In this case, the Author attribute encapsulates an Author object, which is wholly embedded in the owning type and does not exist independently. Compare this to the corresponding diagram in the prior chapter, where the Author object was independent, and existed outside the bounds of the owning object.

In reality, the "captive" distinction is likely logical, not actual, and is simply enforced by the UI. In almost all cases I can imagine, the embedded object is going to be an actual, independent content object in the repository, since a CMS isn't going to create a subsystem of object management solely for typed attributes.

However, with a typed attribute, the UI will not allow you to work with that object anywhere other than in the context of its owning object. Therefore, for all intents and purposes, that's the only place it "lives."

The value of an embedded object is in editorial usability and repository management, since the editorial element will often be an embedded object creation interface specifically for the embedded type. This "sub-interface" might be a modal dialog, collapsible pane, or simple appear as a section inside the main editing interface.

Some editing interfaces might get complicated as the embedded object might be of a type with a very complicated interface itself – in theory, the editing interface of the embedded type could be more complicated than the interface of the owning type.

And what if the embedded object type *also* has attributes which are embedded objects? What if one of those typed attributes requires a type of the owning object... which also requires a value of the embedded type? Could we have an infinitely nested interface?

If the embedded object's UI isn't part of the owner object's UI, then it's still likely be clearly referenced which is helpful for editors. Also, the embedded object should always exist in the same editorial lifecycle – when it's owner is saved, submitted, published, and deleted, the same will occur for the embedded object.

As with referential properties, all other attribute features should still apply:

1. The attribute value can be validated

2. The attribute value can be repeated, if the type allows it

Ideally, validation would operate on two levels. There's an "outer" validation for the type of the owning object, and then an "inner" validation for the type of the embedded object.

The outer validation might enforce that the value is required, and enforce repeating limits (no more than 10, for example). The inner validation would be whatever the type of the embedded object requires.

And either of these validation events could be subject to custom rules. The embedded type (the "inner" validation) might have custom rules to govern its own attributes, and the owning type (the "outer" validation) might have custom rules that reach into the embedded object and inspect its values.

In many cases, the line between a *typed* attribute and a *custom* attribute can get blurry.

Say we want a grouped editorial element for image selection, so when we add an Image attribute to a type, the editor is presented with a (1) file selector, (2) alt text input box, (3) caption input box, and (4) image credit input box. We can do this two ways:

1. Create a custom element that displays all those inputs then serialize them for storage

2. Create an Image content type to be used as a typed attribute value

One difference is that our Image type might also be available as a standalone object, in addition to being available as an embedded attribute value. So, we might have multiple, independent Image objects in our repository for various reasons – the site logo, for example – and it's also available as a typed attribute on several content types. That's not possible for custom attributes, because they're not fully realized content types, just custom editorial interfaces and methods of serializing values.

Typed attributes can be helpful to describe a content type more fully. A content object might become a collection of complex, discrete, repeating objects, indexed by attribute. This can be accomplished with referential attributes as well, but in situations where the inner object is a wholly contained "subsidiary" of the outer object, embedded objects can ease editing and prevent extraneous objects from cluttering up the repository.

Evaluation Questions

- Can an attribute value be an embedded content object?
- How is validation applied to a embedded object? Is the embedded object's internal validation executed?
- How are embedded objects edited from the interface?
- Are there any limitations on embedded object nesting? If an embedded object also contains embedded objects, how is this handled?
- Do events that occur on the owning object also occur on the embedded object? Can the embedded object ever trigger an event?

Evaluation Criteria #9

Can custom validation rules be built?

A CMS is framework for future content. It doesn't know what your content looks like in advance, which is why most systems allow the creation of custom content types.

In addition to baseline structure, a system can only make assumptions about how your content should be logically validated. So built-in validation rules have to make guesses and provide as much coverage for whatever situations might come up. There are a lot of patterns in content management, so things like whether a value is required or whether it falls within a range can cover a lot of use cases.

But what if you have something special? Occasionally, you need to validate an attribute value based on something completely specific to your organization or situation. This could be something that no CMS could predict in advance or be expected to support, or it might require access to others systems, specific to your organization.

In these situations, some systems can be configured with **custom validation rules**.

"Configured" might not be the right word in all cases, because in many situations, custom validation will require a developer to write actual code in the language of the CMS, and that executes in the context of the CMS instance. Changing these rules might mean a full code deploy.

One of the prior examples when discussing pattern validation was a product number in a specific format. This can be validated by generic pattern matching, but the system doesn't "understand" what it is – it doesn't know that this is a product or anything about it. All that rule did was verify a string of characters conformed to a specified pattern. You have no idea if the entered value actually corresponds to a product available in your catalog.

What if you wanted to make absolutely sure your editors entered the product number of a *valid* product, meaning one not discontinued or out-of-stock? This means when the editor attempts to save the attribute value, the CMS needs to connect to the product catalog and perform a lookup on the product number.

Are these two separate rules? Meaning, do you need to check if the product number conforms to the correct pattern, and *then* do a lookup in the catalog? Probably not, since the latter assumes the former – if the value is an invalid pattern, it will clearly fail the lookup, so the pattern match might be unnecessary.

Unless your product catalog is stored inside the CMS, or unless the CMS has some installed integration to your system (which would then, by definition, have to be a known, commodity catalog software), no CMS is going to do this out-of-the-box.

As mentioned above, custom validation almost always involves writing executable code in whatever language the CMS is built on (PHP, C#, Java, etc.). More rarely, custom validation might execute client-side (in the browser; so, JavaScript) but this is less common since custom validation often involves contacting some other system to validate the attribute value, and you usually wouldn't do that directly from the browser.

Some systems will allow you to provide both server-side or **client-side validation**, but more commonly, client-side validation simply performs a HTTP callback to the server, where the validation actually executes.

Client-side validation also presents another issue, as validation shouldn't be the sole responsibility of the user interface. Content needs to be validated *whenever a change is attempted*, through whatever method. If we use the API of our CMS to bulk import a bunch of content, we want those validation rules to execute prior to storing the content in the repository – the API should reject content that doesn't pass validation. Bypassing the user interface should not also bypass our validation rules.

The need for custom validation is inversely proportional to the depth of built-in validation rules. The more coverage provided by built-in rules, the less need you'll have for custom validation.

Here are some situations where custom validation might take the place of built-in validation not provided by the system:

- Range validation, often in the forms of minimum or maximum lengths

- Text pattern validation that can't be captured with regular expressions, such as the parsing of HTML or other text constructs

- Non-required format validation, where a specific format is required only if a value is entered

- Logical values unable to be coerced by the interface or otherwise captured by patterns. (For instance, an editor may only select weekdays in a date picker, however there is no way to eliminate weekends as a selectable option in the editorial element.)

- Dependent validation, where the execution of a rule or a logical variable of a rule is dependent on another value in the same set of changes. (For instance, an editor can't specify Open in a New Window unless they have checked Show in Navigation.)

Custom validation is helpful to preserve the resiliency of your content. It's a more advanced feature that depends on some foresight by the CMS developers, and some foundational programming hooks in the system's API.

Sometimes, however, custom validation isn't enough. Instead we want to completely rewrite the attribute's editorial interface and how it stores data. For this step, we need fully custom attributes.

Evaluation Questions

- Can custom validation rules be built?

- How are they enabled – through deployed code or configuration? If through code, do they have complete access to the API and native functions and constructs of the underlying programming language?

- Are they server-side, client-side, or both?

Evaluation Criteria #10

Can custom attribute types be created?

The number of built-in attribute types differs by system, but eventually you might find yourself needing more than what's offered to fill in gaps. Some systems offer the ability to develop completely custom attribute types.

You might need this for several reasons:

- To display a custom editorial element, specific to your situation

- To enable some custom validation rule, not covered by normal custom rule development

- To store some type of compound attribute value

- To communicate with an external system to provide editorial options

Here's an extended example to demonstrate multiple reasons why a custom attribute might be necessary.

Many systems provide color pickers, but what if you had several unique requirements around color selection? A simple RGB color is three numbers, each from 0 to 255. However, let's complicate this with the following requirements:

- You need to display three small text boxes, in a row, with placeholder text for "R", "G", and "B".

- All three boxes need to be numeric values, from 0 to 255. And you need to validate the colors to avoid shades of gray. So all three boxes have to be unique, and not within 20 units of each other. Since this is a subtle rule, you need to display a clear error message if this validation rule is triggered.

- You need to store the value as text in the format "R,G,B" (so, for example: "146,230,50"). When the value is retrieved by a developer for templating or other processing, you need it be a custom C# class of `ColorSelection` with integer properties for `Red`, `Blue`, and `Green`.

- You need to offer an additional dropdown box with several dozen "Recommended Colors," which will be maintained as separate content by your front-end designer. This dropdown will need to populate from the company style guide, stored in another system. Additionally, this dropdown *and* RGB entries cannot exist at the same time. If a value from the dropdown is selected, any existing RGB entries should be removed, and the textboxes disabled.

- Optionally, the editor can also enter a searchable term that describes the color ("deep red"). This will be entered in the search index as the attribute value.

Sound contrived? It's not. I based this example on an actual custom attribute type I was asked to write once. The "Recommended Colors" were the actual colors of the product line, and the ability to manually specify RGB was just in case those colors "didn't match the images."

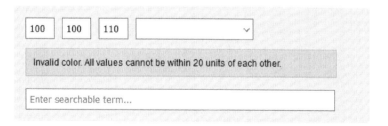

What the described custom attribute type might look like.

Clearly, this is not supported as a built-in attribute type by any existing CMS. The interface and logic around it will have to be built as a custom attribute type.

As we discussed earlier, an attribute is actually a container of several things. For this particular situation, we'd likely need to develop several different units of code:

- The custom editorial element, which would be a combination of HTML, CSS, and JavaScript; the HTML need to be somehow rendered as part of the larger editorial interface, while the custom JavaScript and CSS will usually need to be loaded as external resources

- The custom validation rules

- The custom logical value type

- Serialization code to convert the value type into and out of a primitive value which can be stored (it would likely be stored as structured text: XML or JSON)

- Custom indexing code, to get the alternate value into the search index

API support for custom attributes varies greatly. In a well-architected system, the *built-in* attributes would use an API framework that's designed to be extended, meaning all attributes are "custom" to the extent that they're built using the same framework. This is also helpful as the built-in attribute types provide a pattern on which to base your custom attribute types.

In addition to providing reference implementations, a common framework often allows custom attribute types to **inherit** from built-in attribute types.

For example, if you need some type-ahead search suggestions in a simple text box, it might be helpful to start with a textbox attribute type and extend it by just adding the required JavaScript code, without having to re-implement the entire "attribute bundle," as described above. In many cases, you'll find that your custom attribute is just a built-in attribute with a few selected changes.

> I worked with some editors who wanted a simple code editor, quickly. I did this by extending a textarea attribute type and adding some inline CSS and JavaScript hooks. I called it The Poor Man's Code Editor[1].

Another assumption is that once developed, the custom attribute type is added to the "palette" of attribute types available to use in other content types. A sys-

---

1. *https://gist.github.com/deanebarker/f1c2542b3a510eb992c76c7e07c2f16b*

tem would limit itself considerably if an attribute type could only be developed to service a specific attribute assignment, and would have to be re-implemented for usage in other types.

One school of thought says the perfect CMS wouldn't need custom attribute type development because all necessary types would be provided as built-in. However, this would likely require an attribute type range that would be unreasonably expansive and unwieldy. The next best option, then, is a well-thought out architecture for custom types, and the ability to inherit from and deeply customize existing types.

Evaluation Questions

- Can custom attribute types be created?
- By what method are attribute types created?
- Can built-in attribute types be extended with extra functionality?
- How are the client-side editorial interfaces created? What limitations exist on custom HTML, JavaScript, and CSS? Are there standard frameworks (React, Angular, JQuery, etc.) that will need to be used?

Evaluation Criteria #11

Can attribute values repeat?

Occasionally, an attribute might have more than one value. In a prior chapter, for example, I mentioned storing the names of my children:

- Alec
- Gabrielle
- Isabella

These are three distinct strings of text. If you had a single attribute called "Children," how would you store these?

You could simply put them in a simple text attribute, separated by some sort of marker (technically called a **delimiter**), like this:

- Alec, Gabrielle, Isabella

We discussed this in the chapter on as something called "serialization." In that instance the system was serializing a complex value into a simple one. In this instance, the human editor is doing the serialization. This the three separate values that a human is manually serializing into one.

This has limitations. If you wanted to work with the names separately, you'd have to retrieve this information, break up the text string on the commas and remove the whitespace. And, of course, you'd have to know in advance the delimiter was a comma, and all the editors would need to agree on this. If some-one went rogue and did this –

- Alec | Gabrielle | Isabella

– then we'd have an invalid value. (Actually, we'd technically still have a valid value – since there are no commas, it would deserialize as a single "name" of "Alec | Gabrielle | Isabella".)

You could, of course create three different attributes:

- Child 1
- Child 2
- Child 3

But this assumes you're always going to have three children. What if you have four? What if you have 12?

To improve the editorial experience and the resiliency of our model, you need to establish that each child has a name which is a distinct string of text, and this string can *repeat* a number of times.

This is a **repeating attribute value** or a **multi-valued attribute**. Note the us-age of "value" in those terms. It's not the *attribute* that's repeating. You still have a single attribute, it just has multiple *values*.

A repeating list of dates in Episerver. The "+" sign at the bottom allows you to add a new value. The drag handles to the left of each value allow you to re-order the val-ues. The dropdown menu on the right of each value allow you to delete the value.

What you're modeling here is a "one to many" relationship, which is quite common in traditional relational database modeling. In our case we have *one* logical entity, related to *many* other logical entities. (Note that we're talking about simple text strings in our example, but we could just as easily be talking about a referential attribute which points to other content objects.)

Not every system supports repeating attribute values, as they deeply complicate the underlying data model. Every CMS is supported by some data storage system, which is usually a relational database. Repeating properties can be a very hard thing to retrofit onto an existing system, so they're something that usually has to be planned and implemented very early in a system's development, not added at a later date.

Ideally, repeating attribute values are universal property of attributes, and available for *any* attribute type. For instance, consider our custom color picker from the last chapter. What if we wanted to specify a variable list of available colors for each product in our catalog – some might only have one, and others might have dozens.

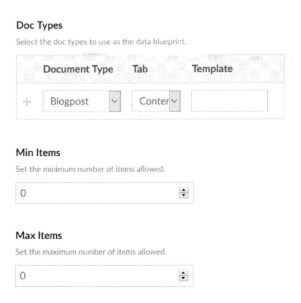

Umbraco allows repetition of entire embedded content types.

Less helpful are specific repeating types, such as an attribute type for "List of Text." Clearly, there are some situations where that works, such as in our example above. But we wanted to store a list of anything other than text, we need to enter and store it as text, which might work (technically, *anything* can be stored as a sequence of characters), but it couldn't be validated or sorted as its logical data.

It's helpful if the system offers specific validation around the characteristics of the repetition. These rules simply dictate the number of values allowed – do we have to have at least one? Is there a maximum number of values, or are they unlimited? Does each value have to be unique?

In addition to validation around the repetition, normally validation over *any one single value* should still apply. If a value is required or needs to conform to a regex pattern, that rule should still execute on each value in our list.

A further step up in functionality is if you can repeat *sets* of attributes. For example, what if you wanted to store the child's date-of-birth, rather than just their name? You now have two distinct attributes for each child:

- Name (text string)
- Date of Birth (date)

You now need to repeat both of those, *grouped together*. You could just have two repeating attributes, and know that the first Name value matches the first Date of Birth value, but that's brittle – what if we somehow get three Name values but only two Date of Birth values?

What you need to do is have each value consist of two distinct attribute values – Name and Date of Birth – as a set.

Show row weights

COMBO:

+

    Combo Field 1

    Combo Field 2

    (Remove)

    Combo Field 1

+

    Combo Field 2

    (Remove)

(Add another item)

The Drupal module Field Collection allows for sets of attributes (which are called "Fields" in Drupal) to be grouped into repeating sets.

You might be thinking back to the chapter on referential attributes or the chapter on embedded objects and thinking: "at this point, child should become a separate content type!" You're not wrong, and that's another valuable feature – the system should allow the repetition of typed and referential values, so we could model these as embedded or referred Child types, and just have a repeating number of them.

Finally, the ordering of values often matters. Referring back to the children example – the order that the children appears in the list might matter, as it might represent their relative dates of arrival. So, Alec needs to be appear *before* Gabrielle (he is, in fact, seven years older than she is).

I don't think you'll find a system that ignores order in repeating attribute values. Editorial interface support is helpful here, primarily in the form of drag-and-drop re-ordering. If you made a mistake and entered information out of order, it's helpful to be able to simply drag it into the correct order, rather than re-entering data.

Similarly, if you need to remove a value from the middle of a list, it's helpful to be able to simply delete that value, rather than having to move everything below it "up" one step (and potentially leave a blank value at the bottom).

Also helpful would be automatic ordering of values – alphabetically or numerically, for instance. This might be complicated by complex attribute types – how would you order a list of Article objects, or a list of referential attributes, for instance? What if not every object or reference in the list is the same type, so they all have different attributes? More commonly, repeating attributes are retrieved and placed into order in typed object or templating code.

The capability for repeating attribute values is not as common as it should be, given its utility. If it exists, it's often in a limited form (example: "List of Text"). The lack of this feature often results in awkward workarounds.

Evaluation Questions

- Can attribute values repeat?
- Can any attribute type allow repeating values, or is this restricted to specific repeatable attributes (i.e. – "List of Text")?
- Can validation be specified around the nature of the repetition? Can minimums and maximums be specified?
- How is required validation handled for a repeating attribute? Does a single value satisfy the required validation?
- Can sets of attributes be repeated together, as a single unit?
- Can repeating attribute values be ordered? How is this ordering presented and managed in the editorial interface? Can values be removed from the middle of the list of values?
- Can derived ordering rules be specified on attribute values?

Evaluation Criteria #12

Can types be formed through inheritance or composition?

Content models sometimes get large and unwieldy over time – lots of types, with lots of attributes. Remember, content models need to be manageable. I've seen models with multiple dozen content types, each with dozens of attributes many of which are repeated on multiple other types, and the whole thing is so complex that editors have little idea of what content goes where and types are poorly differentiated from each other.

Two features can help you manage this by centralizing attributes into manageable units which can be combined to form types.

Here's a simple fact: a lot of your content types will be very similar. Look at the content model behind the average website, and you'll find a *lot* of types with a Title and a Body attribute. In fact, this is often the built-in model, and types are differentiated only in the ways they *differ* from this built-in model.

- Add a Date Published and an Author and you have an Article or Blog Post
- Add an Industry selector and you have a Case Study

- Add a File Upload you have a White Paper

It could be said, then, that every content type *inherits* the built-in model. A content type isn't built from scratch. It starts off with the attributes from the built-in model, and adds additional attributes to differentiate itself. This is helpful because you often don't need to duplicate Title and Body on every content type.

What if you could further inherit types from your own custom types? This is a concept called **type inheritance**.

Say you decide that every page on your website – whether it be a Text Page, a Press Release, or an Employee Bio – should have an additional tab of attributes for Description and Keywords to represent information that will be rendered as META tags on the page.

You could, of course, just add these to every content type. However, what if you wanted to add some additional SEO attributes later on – like a ROBOTS meta value, or some Open Graph or Twitter Card meta? You'd then have to manually add these to all the types as well.

A more manageable way to handle this would be to create a type for Web Page which includes all these attributes, then *inherit all the other types from that*. So, Web Page type inherits the built-in model, and Simple Text Page, Press Release, and Employee Bio inherit from Web Page, getting all the attributes of both before they even add any attributes of their own.

An inheritance relationship is "active," meaning the attributes are not just copied onto the child type at the time of creation, but rather the child type has a real-time link back to the parent type from which it is inherited, and anything added to the parent type is also instantly available in the child type.

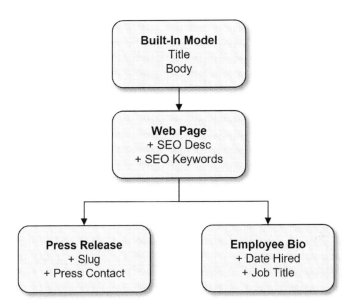

In this example, our Built-in Model has Title and Body. Web Page inherits from that and adds SEO Desc and SEO Keywords. Then both Press Release and Employee Bio inherit from that, and add properties of their own. Both Employee Bio and Press Release have their own attributes plus Title, Body, Desc, and Keywords.

Using inheritance, you can drastically reduce the number of attributes you need on each type. You can "lift out" common attributes and move them "up" to parent types which are inherited, and maintain these common attributes from the top down.

Your content types now exist in a tree of increasing specificity. At the top is the built-in model which represents the most general content (and which might never actually be used directly; more on that below), and below that are types which incrementally add attributes. The type tree branches out to provide specific attribute inheritance to different groups of types.

While inheritance is absolutely helpful, it does have drawbacks. Logically, types can only have *one* parent. It can be tricky if you have attributes that need to inherit down multiple branches of a type tree.

Consider our example from above. What if you decided that a lot of content has a set of Contact attributes – a Contact Name, Phone Number, etc. You want this for our Press Release type, but also for other types like our Case Study and

Legislative Action types.

Great, just add an interstitial type under Web Page for ... Content with Contact Information ... and then you can put a bunch of types under that.

Later, you decide that a bunch of types are date- and location-specific, meaning they have a Start Date and an optional End Date, along with a Location Name and Location Coordinates. So you decide to create... Content with Location Information ... and put other types under that.

However, then you realize that Press Release really needs *both* of those things. How can you maneuver it to inherit from both of them?

The underlying problem is this: with type inheritance, *you can only have one path back up the tree*, and your type will "collect" all the attributes it finds on that path. This is sometimes exactly what you want, but sometimes it isn't and you can get locked into a weird place.

> Programmers run into this exact same problem with object oriented programming. Classes can inherit from other classes, and it's tricky when you want things from *two* parents. It *is* possible in some languages (called, appropriately, "multiple inheritance"), but it's not common because it can get complicated.

What can often be more helpful than inheritance, is the concept of **type composition**.

Content types are often composed of pre-defined sets of attributes. Think of it like a buffet – you walk around with your plate, and you take a little from here, and a little from here, and eventually you have a full plate. Your plate hasn't inherited from anything – it starts out completely empty. You've just "composed" a full plate out of different things you find on the buffet line.

Composition encourages you to group your attributes into sets that serve a specific purpose, then compose a type from (1) its own, unique attributes, and (2) additional sets of attributes that serve additional purposes.

Sets of related attributes are effectively "free floating" and not locked into a tree. They can be injected into any type when necessary.

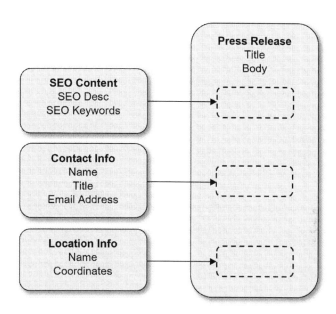

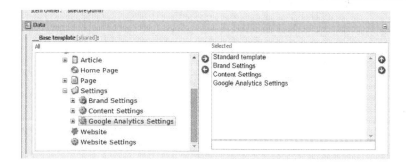

When dealing with inheritance or composition, you're expanding the boundaries of your types to encompass other types and groups of attributes. This can cause problems if not monitored carefully.

It's helpful for a system to differentiate between "public types" and "support types." There will be some types that editors are expected to create objects from (Press Release, for example), and others that exist only to enhance other types (Location Info, for example).

An editor shouldn't be able to directly create the latter. Some of this can be handled through model access permissions, but a system might have another method to specify that a type is solely meant to support inheritance or composition, and is never intended to be the source type for an object.

> In object-oriented programming, this is known as an "abstract class." I've never known a CMS to refer to an "abstract type," but the analogy fits.

You also need to beware of circular references. If B inherits from A, you need to somehow make sure that A didn't inherit from B, or else you have a circular reference and when the system tries to crawl up the type tree, it's going to run around in circles. The same thing could theoretically happen in composition. If B incorporates A, then A cannot incorporate B. Hopefully, a system has some method for preventing this.

Finally, you need to be more careful with type changes, because they can have vastly magnified effects. If you've injected SEO Info into 90% of your other types, and someone decides Press Releases don't need Keywords anymore, then deletes that attribute... well, Very Bad Things might happen. When every type has its own attributes, then type changes are localized. When you start inheriting or compositing types, type changes become systemic, sometimes with disastrous results.

Type inheritance and composition can *vastly* improve the manageability of any content model. Inheritance is absolutely better than no inheritance. However, in my experience, composition is the more useful tool overall.

Evaluation Questions

- Can custom content types be inherited or extended from existing types?
- Can custom content types be composed by active inclusion of pre-configured sets of attributes?
- Can content types or attribute sets be configured in such a way that they exist only for inheritance and composition, and cannot be the direct source for a new object?
- Are there any safeguards against circular references?

Evaluation Criteria #13

Can content objects be organized into a hierarchy?

We've talked a bit about relationships between content objects via referential attributes. But there's another object relationship so common it's frequently built-in as a core feature: a parent-child relationship, in the form of an overarching **content tree**.

> More accurately, this should be an "object tree," but "content tree" is commonly used.

A content tree is a group of content objects organized into a hierarchy. One content object is the **content root**, and it contains one or more child objects, each of which might also have child objects, and so on "down" the tree.

> Yes, yes, I know – it's really an upside down tree, when visualized, which means when we talk about moving "up" or "down" the tree, it might be confusing. The

content root is at the top, and levels visually open downward, which isn't how an actual tree works, but the nomenclature has stuck.

Parent-child relationships are quite common:

- A Book object has multiple Chapter child objects
- A Department object has multiple Faculty Member child objects
- A Recipe object has multiple Ingredient child objects
- A Page object has multiple Page child objects

Generally speaking, parent-child relationships are how humans organize concepts. We move from broad concepts to more narrow concepts. A lot of our content is organized the same way.

⊿ 📄 About

    ⊿ 📄 Governance and Leadership

        📄 Board of Trustees for Sanford Health

        📄 Executive Leadership

    ⊿ 📄 Community Benefit

        📄 Community Benefit Annual Report

      ▶ 📄 Community Benefit Awards

        📄 Community Care Program

    ▶ 📄 Community Health Needs Assessment

An object tree in Sitecore. In that image are nine separate content objects, organized into a hierarchy with three distinct levels.

What a content gives us are multiple implicit relationships for every content object:

- An object can be related to one or more **child objects**
- Every object (except the content root) is related to a single **parent object**
- An object might also be related to **sibling objects** – children of the same parent

- Objects are often said to be "above" another object (closer to the content root), or "below" another object (further from the content root)

- Objects above an object (so, closer to the content root) are said to be **ancestors** of the object (one of them is both the parent and an ancestor)

- Objects below an object (so, further from the content root) are said to be **descendants** (child objects are both children and descendants).

- An object together with its descendants is often called a **branch** of the tree. (Occasionally, a content object with no children will be called a **leaf** or a **leaf node**.)

- Objects might also have a behavioral relationship with objects at the same **depth** or **level** as themselves, defined as their distance from the content root. For example, objects directly under the content root are often considered to be at a depth of 1, while their aggregate child objects (so all the children of all objects at depth 1) are considered to be at a depth of 2, etc.

- Objects directly under the content root are often called **top level** objects. (In web-based systems, "top level pages" is often used to refer to objects directly under the home page, regardless of that depth relative to the content root.)

What can be odd is that this is a rare case when the *objects* define the model, not necessarily *types*. So far, we've been talking about the structure that has arisen from content and attribute types. With a content tree, we're discussing the structure that arises from creating actual objects and organizing them.

It's actually quite natural, since the tree effectively creates two pseudo-attributes on every object. If any content can be organized hierarchically, then every type effectively has a referential attribute for Parent and a repeating referential attribute for Children. The tree just builds those in.

> In fact, if your system doesn't support a tree, you absolutely can fake one – create actual attributes for Parent and Children. However, you would likely need to recreate a lot of the tree-based functionality that's built-in to systems that support trees natively, and the editorial UI would be deeply uncomfortable to work with.

It's important to note that a content tree is not a **folder tree**. Some systems attempt to organize content into a series of "folders," much like a computer operating system. This is done with the idea that folders are intuitive to end users.

However, what this model misses is that *a folder is usually not a content object*. It's some other data construct, that doesn't act like a content object. For instance, it can't be the operative object of inbound URL requests, and it often has completely different (or omitted) functionality for permissions, versioning, and workflow.

Additionally, if a folder is the *only* thing that can contain content, then you lose all the modeling capabilities of parent-child relationships. The only implicit relationship a folder tree offers is a sibling relationship of a content object with all the other objects in the same folder.

If you have a object tree, but your situation absolutely requires the concept of "folders," then you're usually able to just fake it – create a Folder type, give it a Name attribute, and allow it to contain child objects of all kinds. If your system allows it, you can even change the icon to something that looks like a folder. For many situations, this works just fine, and you still have all the aforementioned relational benefits.

> I was talking to a vendor once about their content tree. I asked if it was based on folders and they quickly responded, "Whoa, whoa. Never say the 'F' word around us..."

A content tree presents a natural user interface for editors. The tree is usually visually represented, and editors can open and close branches of the tree to drill down into descendants. Moving your focus up and down a tree is called **traversal**.

Most tree-based systems offer a way to create child objects under another object (provided the editor has sufficient permissions) via a "Create Content Here" button or something similar.

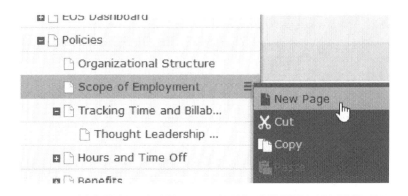

Episerver pages organized into a tree, with a "New Page" link to create new content underneath the selected parent (a page called "Scope of Employment," in this example). Episerver also includes "Cut" and "Copy" options to allow the "pasting" content somewhere else, in addition to drag-and-drop object movement.

Many systems will also offer drag-and-drop functionality to move content objects from one parent to another.

Back when we discussed type inheritance and composition, we talked about some problems with conceptual trees. That discussion was in the context of a type inheritance tree, but the same base problem is true of a content tree – an object can only have *one* parent, and sometimes this can be a problem.

For example, it's very common to have a tree of Page objects to model web navigation. Hierarchical navigation is extremely common in websites. For example, the home page has a child page of "Products" which has multiple child pages, one for each product, each of which might have other child pages for other information. This tree structure is used to format and display navigation menus and crumbtrails – the links are created by traversing the tree from the origin point of whatever content the user is viewing.

What if a page needs to appear in more than one place? What if the navigation menu next to *every* product needs to include a link to download the same whitepaper? If you're generating navigation directly from the content tree, this can get complicated. Do you create the same download page as a child of every project page? And when the page changes, do you just need to update it in every location?

Ideally, you can have the same content appear in more than one place in the same tree. This is often possible through the use of **object references**. An object reference is – wait for it – an object that references another object. So, you create your whitepaper download page in one place, then create a reference object everywhere else you want the page to appear, all of which point back to the original object. Changes can be made to the original object, and since the references don't have any content of their own and just point back to the original object, they'll all update.

There are two ways these reference objects might work –

1. The reference object might actually transport the user across the tree. So, clicking on a reference object to our original whitepaper object might take the user to that original object. So the page appears in more than one location for the purposes of navigation, but it can only be viewed in its original location.

2. The reference object might allow viewing in its reference location, *as if the original was located there all along.*

Some systems offer both options, which is helpful. Each solution has its advantages and drawbacks, and there are use cases for both.

> Under the hood, many object trees are actually trees of "nodes." A node is nothing but a reference to a single content object. Each node has a parent and some children which form a tree in aggregate, and each node is linked to a single content object. The trick is that *more than one node can link to the same content object.*
>
> Nodes can only appear in one place in the tree, but *every* node could theoretically link to the *same* content object, resulting in a tree appearing be comprised solely of the same object (which, it must be said, would be pointless, but it illustrates the point).
>
> This concept of nodes and objects is usually always hidden from users and editors – to them, the tree is just objects.

Some systems offer **typed trees**, whereby the parent-child relationships can be limited by type. Consider some of our examples from above:

*   A Recipe can be a parent to an Ingredient, but an Ingredient should never be a parent to a Recipe.

*   A Quiz can have multiple Question children, but the inverse isn't true. Additionally, Question objects aren't allowed child objects of any type.

By default, some systems allow all types as children of all other types, while other systems allow no children of any type. In both cases, you need to configure the type to allow certain kinds of objects, or disallow others. Systems of both kinds operate on either exclusion or inclusion – you configure a type to *allow* specific child types, assuming all other types are *disallowed*, or vice-versa.

When a tree is typed, object creation options are limited. When an editor is presented with a type selection interface, the list of types will be filtered to only those types available for creation under the parent context.

> When multiple types can be created, the creation option is usually something like "Create Content" or "New Content" which leads to a menu to select the type from which to create your new object.
>
> However, when only one type is allowed as a child of a particular parent, many systems will change the label to be type-specific – "Create Page" or "New Ingredient" – and skip the now-superfluous type selection screen altogether.

A typed tree is a form of value coercion. Remember, a child relationship is really an implicit attribute on both sides – the child gets a referential attribute to its parent, and the parent gets a repeating, referential attribute representing its children. Rather than evaluating an input after the fact, a typed tree imposes coercive validation by parentage – it prevents an invalid attribute value from even being initiated.

Beyond modeling, a content tree often influences other functionality and how it applies to various objects. A parent-child relationship implies some level of control from the parent over the child, and it's common for systems to allow functionality to inherit down the tree.

Permissions, for example – in many systems, a child object will inherit the permission set of its parent, in one of two ways:

1. The parent's permission set is copied into the child object when it's created

2. The child has no permission set, and instead actively refers to its parent when its permissions are referenced. This is is generally preferable, since the child's permissions will mirror the parent's permissions and change in parallel.

Other functionality that might filter from parent child to child are approval sequences, ancestral URL paths, and notification options.

Like we discussed with , this can cause unintended, systemic effects. Changing the settings on a single object can cascade all sorts of changes down that branch of the tree.

Never is this more true than with tree-based URLs. Change a single URL segment on an object with many descendants, and you might have just changed the URLs for *thousands* of content objects. This threat is so common that some systems have code built specifically to catch this and automatically create redirects for all the objects that now have different URLs.

Cascading attribute values is a pattern that's inherent in tree-based organization. You can traverse the tree to find inherited attribute values that would cascade to a starting node on the tree. So, these are values inherited by an object by virtue of its position in the content tree.

In effect, attributes can cascade their values "down" the tree to the objects below them. Any attribute on any object can be accessed by all its descendants, causing that attribute to apply to an entire branch of the tree.

Consider a Section type, meant to represent a collection of pages in a website about a specific topic ("Products" for example). There might be dozens of Page objects as the nested descendants of a Section.

The Section has an attribute for Section Banner. If you wanted each of those pages to display the banner indicating what section they existed in, you can retrieve this by detecting the page's position in the tree.

Remember that a Page will have an implicit reference to a Section by virtue of being its descendant. To find the owning section, you simply need to "crawl up the tree" from the Page that is being displayed toward the content root, until you find a Section. The first Section object found is, by definition, the section in which that particular page resides, and you can read the Section Banner attribute from that object and display it.

This means every Page object has an implicit Section Banner positional attribute. It also means that moving a page underneath another Section object will change the displayed banner, since a different Section object will be now found when searching toward the content root.

For web-based systems, the tree often represents a hierarchy of URL-addressable web pages. A common pattern is for the content root to be the home page, and other pages will branch out below it. This makes sense, as the tree model overlays nicely onto web navigation.

However, it can be helpful to not *require* the content root to be the home page of a particular website, for a couple reasons.

First, in multi-site environments, you'll have more than one home page. In these cases, the content root is a more abstract type of content object (often just called "Root"), with multiple home pages as children. The content root literally just represents the "parent" of all content. It's often its own type, which can be helpful to store attributes that should cascade to multiple websites (things like legal disclaimer text, API key values, etc.)

> Some systems even allow you to define a new website at *any* point on the tree. So, from the content root, you might descend multiple organizational levels before you get to a content object that represents a home page. Its descendants would represent pages of that website. Requests to that site's domain would "enter" the tree at that object.

Second, in systems that don't have a model for non-page content, it's handy to have an area "hidden" from the URL scheme.

In web systems, a content object's URL is often formed from its position in the tree, *relative to the home page*, which means something that isn't a descendant of the home page won't get a URL (or, it might get an invalid URL that doesn't actually return content).

In these situations, you might have an object at the same level as the home page (so, a sibling of the home page), under which you "hide" this non-page content. The content would be injected into delivery contexts (again, we'll talk about that term later) via code in a template or delivery context.

A content tree can be a rich source of intention and meaning. Just creating a content object as the child of another object establishes a relationship that can be referenced, traversed, and leveraged to allow functionality, access, and formatting.

Evaluation Questions

- Does the system have a built-in object tree? If not an object tree, does it have a folder tree?

- Does the tree support typing restrictions? How are these typing restrictions presented in the editorial UI?

- Is it possible for the same content object to effectively appear in two locations in the tree?

- If a web-based system, is the root object in the tree always the home page?

- What functionality is derived by placement in the tree? What functionality is cascading down from parentage?

- If a web-based system, are URLs formed by tree placement?

- Is there any built-in support for cascading attribute values, from ancestor to descendant?

- What methods of tree traversal and querying are available from the API?

Evaluation Criteria #14

Can content objects inherit from other content objects?

We've discussed the idea of , where we base one type on another. The *inheriting* type gets all the attributes of the *inherited* type, then adds some more of its own.

Sometimes, its helpful to have content *object* inheritance, where a object can inherit from another fully populated object, and maintain a reference back to it. Instead of the configuration of attributes, what's being inherited are the actual attribute *values*.

> To make this easier to discuss, we're going to use "base" to refer to the *inherited* object, and "derived" to refer to the *inheriting* object. It's tempting to lean on parent-child nomenclature, but after our discussion of object trees, that means something else and can make this discussion confusing.

In this model, attribute values for the derived object can override attribute values for the base object. Put another way, when values aren't provided for the derived object, the base values will "bubble up."

Imagine a base content object with its attribute labels and values printed on a piece of paper. Lay that piece of paper on a flat surface, then print another content object out in the same format. For values you want to inherit from the base object, simply cut them out of the second paper, leaving holes where they were. Lay the second object on top of the first, and some values from the base object will show through the holes, while others will be covered up.

Effectively, the base object provides default attribute values which can change in real-time. The derived object – which is sometimes called a **variation** – overrides those values when desired.

This can be helpful for channel-specific renditioning.

For example, if you want to publish your Article objects into a mobile app, you might want to change some attribute values to accommodate a smaller viewing area. You could create another Article object which overlays on our base article and becomes a variation for mobile. It might only supply an alternate value for Title, which hides the base title. All other attribute values should source from the base object.

This might seem similar to supplying a default value for an attribute, with one important difference – with variations, the link is active, and the defaults are provided when the object is retrieved from the repository. If values change on the base object at any time, the inherited values will changes on the derived object.

Back to our example from above – the Subtitle attribute value would source from the base object, since no value was provided in the variation. We can change this base subtitle – even *years* later – and that change will be reflected in real-time in the variation. Conversely, a default value would be populated when the derived object was created, and would then become just like any other attribute value on the object, never having any link back to the base object.

Localization and **personalization** can also be achieved by use of derived object.

For the former, a content object can exist in a default language, and derived variations of that object for each language could be "overlaid" on top of it. The derived object might supply new values for some attributes which need to be translated – like the Title. Other attributes are universal to all languages – Image Alignment, for example – so the values from the base object are used.

In practice, localization is such a core feature of any CMS that there are specific subsystems built for it, but it illustrates the value that object inheritance provides: some objects are just mildly altered versions of other objects, customized slightly for a specific use case.

This is doubly true with personalization. We might have a Case Study object explaining how our new high-efficiency furnace cuts heating costs. Normally, the Image accompanying the text is of a single-family home. However, if we detect the user is visiting from mid-town Manhattan, we want to swap that image out for one of a brownstone.

In this case, we might create a derived variation of our case study where the only new attribute value supplied was the Image. Every other attribute value is the same.

> What we're not discussing here is how a specific visitor is "matched" to a derived object that provides the correct personalization or language requirement. This would be part of the delivery context, and is beyond the scope of this chapter.

Object inheritance gets logically difficult when trying to "void" an attribute value on the base object. The base object provides a Subtitle and you don't want one for your derived object, how do you specify that? Not specifying a value for Subtitle would naturally be interpreted as wanting the base value to bubble up. How do you provide a value which is... no value?

> I don't mean to be enigmatic about this point, but I have never seen an explicit method of handling this.

By the same token, object inheritance clearly provides some challenges around validation, particularly with required values. It's quite common for Title to be required, so any system offering this as a feature would need to provide options for circumventing validation when an object is inherited from a base.

If object inheritance is not offered by a system, it can often be hacked in at the API or template level in the specific cases when it's needed. You might see a "base object" loaded alongside the desired object, and code executed to fill missing attributes from the base object.

At the template level, something as simple as an `if...then` construct could display data from a "base" object when the operative object didn't provide a value.

However, as noted in the prior section, validation gets complicated. If your system is ignorant of object inheritance, then it will blindly enforce all validation rules on your derived object, which makes overriding just one or two attributes very difficult.

Object inheritance is not particularly common, but can be very helpful in (1) highly granulated scenarios, where content is deeply customized for specific delivery requirements, or (2) high-volume scenarios, where large amounts of similar content need a set of default values that can be updated in real-time.

Evaluation Questions

- Can objects inherit values from a base object?
- Is it possible to void/nullify an attribute value on the derived object when that value is provided by the base object?
- How is validation affected or circumvented in the derived object?
- Is the reference to the base object subject to dependency management or referential integrity checks?

Evaluation Criteria #15

What is the relationship between "pages" and "content"?

> Be aware that this chapter goes off on some tangents. It may seem to be about everything *but* modeling, but the concepts presented here are important to understand the modeling paradigms of a web-centric CMS.
>
> And while the title implies web-centricity, there's information here that applies to multiple contexts. The web is simply a channel, and other channels will operate on similar paradigms as those required to generate templated content for a web page.

The concept of (1) a content object existing in a web content management system, and (2) that content object getting a URL at which it can be retrieved, are two separate things. However, in some systems they get combined. Understanding the relationship between a page and a content object is critical to deciding how content gets modeled.

In older systems, the idea of "pages" was often not even part of the CMS. Pages were just executable templates on the file system that pulled content into them. This gave us URLs like:

```
/article.php?id=42
```

In that case, the executable file called "article.php" was acting as the page and the content was a database record with a key of "42". They were combined at request time, and the result was sent back as the HTTP response.

In this example, the content has no concept of a page. It doesn't even know it's being rendered into a page. It's just pure data that happens to be pulled into a page rendering process at request time.

In fact, the CMS itself (insofar as a raw database is acting as a CMS) doesn't even have any concept of the page. The request for `article.php` is handled by the web server. It processes the logic of responding to the request, which just happens to involve contacting a database for information.

Later, CMSs started managing the actual concept of the page itself. Pages became virtual and were no longer represented by a file on disk that was the direct target of a URL request. This seems routine now, but at the time (think, turn of the century), it was ground-breaking. It also led to the idea of "pages" and "content" getting mashed together.

Now, the CMS itself is much more intimately involved in the request process. The CMS knows that its responding to an HTTP request, and it becomes involved in the URL interpretation and content mapping required to match content with that request.

This requires a CMS to be "page aware" – or perhaps more accurately, "URL aware" – and it means there's some link between a URL and a content object. How this link is architected, managed, and maintained is subject to several different patterns.

Distilled down to its core, when we say "page" we really mean "URL," or, even more generally, we mean "address" or even "query." We're talking about a text string to which a specific data construct is assigned and returned (in whatever form) when that string is activated in some way, whether it's entered in a browser address bar, sent over an API, whatever.

As the risk of over-abstraction, this is simply a mapping. A URL is a "ticket" that can be exchanged for something. A data construct is assigned to a specific ticket, and the CMS matches this ticket up when it receives a request.

For most all modern, coupled CMSs, a URL is assigned to a specific content object, whether it be a Page or an Article or a Employee Bio. The **operative content object** is the content object to which a request is directed – this is the content object that the user specifically wants, and that the request primarily operates on.

Consider:

```
/news/politics/2019/08/11/china-trade-war-heats-up
```

That URL is clearly directed to a specific content object – an Article object, from the looks of it. The processing for the request will undoubtedly use other content to some degree, but it's fair to say there's a specific Article object in the repository that's the main intention of this request.

The operative content object is rarely served "raw." Except in headless architectures (discussed below), any response to the request is transformed via some rendering operation, such as a template execution. We'll refer to this combination of (1) URL mapping, (2) operative content object, and (3) and rendering execution in response to a request, as a **delivery context**.

A delivery context is all the processing acrobatics that a CMS goes through to turn raw content into a presentable form that can be delivered to the requestor. In some systems, this might be an MVC controller. In other systems, this might be as simple as the direct access and execution of a PHP or ASP file. In other systems, this might be as simple as retrieving a file from the file system.

The operative content object might not be the *only* object used in that delivery context. It's common for other objects to be "recruited" to fulfill a request, in two ways:

1. The operative content object might refer to other objects via referential attributes

2. The rendering template might query the repository and display information from other objects

The resulting request is therefore usually an aggregation of content; we'll call this the **content payload**.

A common sequence looks like this:

1. The CMS intercepts the inbound HTTP request (and thereby prevents the web server from just serving from the file system)

2. The CMS determines and retrieves the operative content object to which the request is directed

3. The CMS determines how that object needs to be transformed, often by finding a root template to execute

4. The CMS creates and executes a delivery context of some kind; this is usually some controlling code execution and/or cascading templating execution that assembles and transforms a content payload

5. The CMS sends the result of the delivery context back as an HTTP response

The specifics will vary from system to system, but the above is quite common.

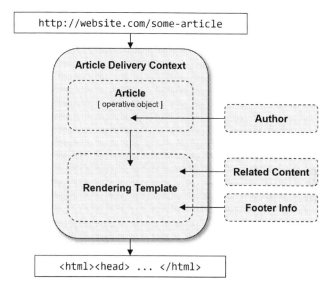

The delivery context is the operation required to assemble and transform the content payload. In this example, a URL has mapped to an Article object as its operative content object.

The delivery context to fulfill this request recruits other content, either through referential attributes on the operative object (Author) or delivery context-driven operations, like the retrieval of related content and footer information through controller or templating code. The result of the delivery context is sent back as the response to the original request.

In some systems, the concepts of "page" and "content" are separate things. Pages might not be considered actual content.

In these systems, you often manage pages explicitly, usually in a tree. These are a special data construct designed to represent a web page. In these systems, you sometimes have page-specific information ("META Keywords", "Title Tag", etc.) on the page construct, completely separate from the attributes of the operative content object or content payload that the page delivers.

In these systems, pages get URLs, but *content* is in some separate organizational structure. Content objects get assigned "into" pages. A page therefore "wraps" a content object for delivery – pages are a container for content.

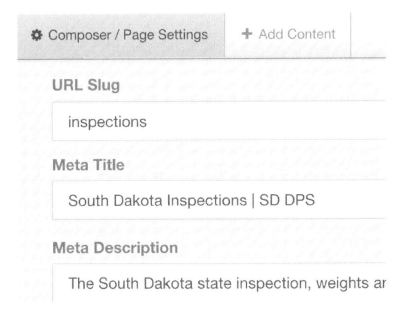

In Concrete5, a page is a distinct structure, apart from the content which appears on that page. Pages contain information specific to the role of a web page, editable in a dialog shown here, but content is added to pages in specific zones (the "Add Content" option at the top).

On the other end of the scale, some systems dictate that content objects *are automatically pages themselves* – the content object gets a URL and is directly addressable as a page.

This "omni page" architecture operates on a spectrum. In some systems *every* content object is like this. Sure, you might be creating a "Person" object, but that's also a page, whether you like it or not. This is common in web-focused systems which are said to be "page-based," meaning every content object gets an addressable URL.

The term **page-based CMS** has become vaguely pejorative over the years, as if to emphasize that a vendor's system is so myopic it can't envision content existing outside of a page. If you ever hear the phrase "page-based CMS," I promise you it wasn't mean as a compliment and was probably tossed out by a competing vendor.

Omni-page architectures are common in web-focused systems with a primary content tree, since the format of a URL overlays nicely on the concept of a tree.

(Consider: a URL is essentially a tree serialized into a text string.) Most tree-based systems will form URLs by assigning a URL segment, and crawling the tree from the content object back to the root, and concatenate these segments into a string.

A page in Episerver, with its URL segment defined. The URL segment is an attribute of the content object, and the URL segments of the page and all its ancestors forms the URL. In Episerver, any type inherited from a specific base type is an addressable page. Episerver has another type of content (a "Block") for content that doesn't get a URL assignment and is therefore not directly addressable.

Really, any content that's assigned a dedicated URL is assumed to be a page. This might not be intended, of course, but if a content object gets assigned a URL, then it can be said to be "page-ish," at the very least. (It doesn't matter what you call it, if it walks like a duck and talks like a duck...)

So, the extremes of this scale are:

1. Systems where pages are a completely separate construct from content

2. Systems where every content object is also a page

In reality, most systems lie somewhere between the two. They'll offer some type of page architecture, but will also have content that doesn't represent pages, and therefore isn't URL addressable. This is preferable to the extremes, since there are times when you might want "pure" content that is never meant to be directly accessed, and other times when you have a large volume of content that *should* be represented in a page construct, so creating a separate page for each is inefficient and tedious.

What we've been discussing above are traditional **coupled CMSs**. A coupled CMS generates a delivery context for every request and performs real-time operations to form a content payload and return the result.

There are two other models that might be considered "time-shifted" delivery contexts. They still create and execute a delivery context, they just do it in advance, save the result, and some other system – usually a simple web server – delivers that result when it's requested in the future.

- A **decoupled CMS** manages content, then generates responses in advance and stores them, normally as a static HTML file

- A **static site generator** does the same thing, but it doesn't actually manage content, it just executes the delivery context against an existing repository

You might say a decoupled CMS is a static site generator with a built-in content repository, or that a static site generator is a delivery context that can connect to an existing content repository. The line gets very blurry.

While saving and delivering the result of a prior delivery context is helpful for lot of reasons (performance, fault tolerance, server load, etc.), it has the drawback that it cannot respond directly to the inbound request. Since there's *one* delivery context that's saved for multiple future requests, you normally cannot alter anything in response to those requests.

A coupled CMS, by comparison, is executing a new delivery context for every request, and can inject variables into it based on things like the identity of the user, their location, their prior activity, and even things like the time of day and background data like current product pricing information.

Additionally, a **headless CMS** actively rejects the delivery context model altogether. It has no controlling code, no template rendering, and no content payload. You request specific content, or a specific query for content, and you get that content back, and nothing else. It's not saving a prior context like a decoupled CMS, it just has no context at all. The content is delivered to "raw," serialized into a structured text format like JSON or XML, directly as it's retrieved from the repository.

So, where does the delivery context happen with a headless CMS? Wherever you decide to build it.

> Note that a few headless CMSs are blurring the lines by offering "HTML as a service," where they can perform some limited templating or transformation on content before returning it.

Part of the understanding when working with a headless CMS is it's only a repository, and you will write a delivery context system to manage things like the URL translation to identify the operative content object, the assembly of the content payload, and any necessary rendering. You write this in a completely separate environment from the headless CMS, in whatever technology stack you like. With headless, there's always another environment somewhere that's actually delivering the content, be it a mobile app, a website, a display ad, etc.

For some clients, this is exactly what they want, since they'd prefer to bring their own tools and architectures to the delivery context, for whatever reason. For other clients, this involves a large amount of work to simply arrive at the same level of functionality that a traditional coupled CMS provides out of the box.

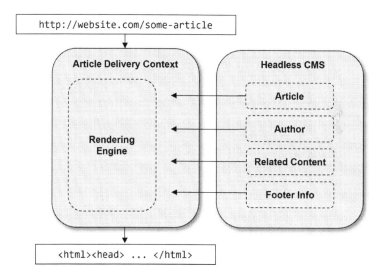

With a headless CMS, the delivery context exists apart from the CMS. The delivery context is developed as a custom app or using a non-CMS framework, and the CMS exists "alongside" it. All URL request translation and content retrieval happens outside of the CMS.

Does this sound familiar? A coupled CMS is *opinionated*, much like we discussed in . The concept of having a delivery context at all is an opinion that the vendor is imposing because it matches the use cases and patterns of most of their customers. There's a good chance you agree with this opinion, but if you don't, you need to find a system that doesn't impose it.

Without a URL, content is sometimes said to be **placeless**, meaning it's not directly addressable – the implication of a URL address meaning it has a "place" and exists in some location relative to a larger context.

Consider blog comments. They aren't normally URL-addressable, and they only exist to be rendered as part of the blog post to which they're assigned. When a new blog comment is entered, it's appropriate to store it as "placeless" content. The only reference a blog comment needs to a larger context is some link back to the post on which it was entered.

Other than that reference, the blog comment can just exist in some big conceptual "bin" of other comments, to be retrieved by its post link when the post is rendered.

To refer back to our prior nomenclature, a blog comment will never be the operative content object of a request. It's never the "main point" of a request – it exists solely to support another content object (the blog post), and it's recruited for this purpose in the delivery context.

As we discussed above, some systems are omni-page to the point where *every-thing* gets an assigned URL, even things you don't want to have a URL (like blog comments, for example).

However, just because a content object gets a URL, you're not absolutely required to deliver it there. A traditional, coupled CMS will resolve the URL back to that content object and deliver the data to a templating layer, but you can technically output anything you want. You control the logic of the template, so you can do whatever you need to do here.

If you have a CMS that *always* assigns a URL for content you never want to be directly addressable, you have a couple options:

1. Your rendering template can just return a 404 (hopefully, an *actual* 404, but if not, then a page that resembles a 404).

2. A request for that content could be redirected to where the content is actually displayed, often in the context of another object. In our blog comment above, the request could return a redirect to the containing blog post (perhaps with a bookmark to scroll down to the actual blog comment).

This entire discussion probably seems like a minor point, and it is...until it isn't. You start a web project thinking about pages, but you'll eventually run into content that doesn't match one-for-one to a URL, or start delivering content to channels that don't have any concept of "pages." For these situations, you need to understand the content/page/URL relationship.

I have seen CMS implementations which have descended into chaos primarily because the relationship between pages and content was deeply misunderstood early in the modeling process.

Evaluation Questions

- What is the coupling model of the CMS: coupled, decoupled, or headless?

- Are pages an explicit construct in the system, separate from content objects, or are all content objects considered pages?

- If not all content is considered a page, then how and why is content assigned or not assigned a URL?

Evaluation Criteria #16

Can access to types and attributes be limited by user permissions?

Not every type and attribute is created equal. They can differ greatly in terms of necessity, complication, and consequences.

Some content types – Text Page or Article – might be ubiquitous and straightforward. Others – Home Page or Image Carousel – might be less so.

The same is true of attributes. The model behind a type isn't a single unit, remember – it's a collection of attributes, and sometimes we can vary access to them individually.

Every editor probably needs access to the Title and Body, but what about the URL Segment or the Suppress Navigation checkbox? Are these things every editor is trained for? Are these things you want every editor to be able to change?

Some systems offer permission-based access to different aspects of the content model. This can be used as a form of coercion – you can promote good editorial practices by preventing editors – by individual or group – from affecting certain types and attributes.

We mentioned above that not every aspect of the content model is created equal, but here's an additional, awkward truth – *not every editor is created equal*. Throughout this text, we've lumped editors together in one group, but there's a wide range.

Bookending the "normal" editor are (1) lighter-weight editors who might only do one thing with the content, and (2) "power" editors, who are quasi-administrators who can do everything with content, and even some configuration and pseudo-development when necessary.

Working with some content types might require additional training. There might be image sizing, format, or focal point considerations; the attributes of the particular object might have far-reaching implications; or changing the value of an attribute – especially in tree-based systems with cascading implications – might risk violating an organizational standard.

This speaks to both content model resiliency and editorial usability. Not only do we want to protect our content, but there's nothing more demoralizing for an editor than inadvertently breaking something they were unaware could break.

Some content types have intentionally limited use. For example, the Home Page. By definition, there's one per website, so there's very few reasons why one would need to be created after site launch. In programming, structures which should only have a single instance are known as **singletons**.

Additionally, in many tree-based systems, a common pattern holds that global properties are modeled and stored on the home page object. This is due to both (1) the singularity of the home page, and (2) the ability for cascading attributes on the content root (which is often the home page) to affect every object in the tree, since everything else is a descendant.

There might be other types that aren't pure singletons but are rarely created post-launch. Entire new sections of the website, for example, might require the creation of a new Section object, but this needs to be accompanied by multiple other changes and content restructuring, or else the website might begin to malfunction. As such, access to the Section type should be limited to a few power editors who would likely be involved in or spearhead a large-scale change such the creation of an entirely new section.

In information security, the "Principle of Least Privilege" dictates that you default to the least amount of access as possible, and only grant expanded access as necessary. This usually yields in the face of practical management to the reality of *groups* of users being dictated *sets* of privileges, but it still applies in principle. Part of a content modeling project is determining who has access to what parts of the model, and this feature of a CMS helps you keep that as tightly constrained as possible.

Many systems will offer **type-level permissions** – permissions for object creation based on type so certain types can be restricted from certain editors.

This is only applicable on object *creation*, since once an object is created, its permissions will revert to those on the object, rather than the type the object is based on (and many times, those permissions will be inherited from its parent). You can't put a permission on something that doesn't exist. So, the only way to control the ability to create an object is to put that permission on the type.

In our home page example, we could simply remove all object creation permissions for the Home Page type once the home page has been created during site development. If no one can create another one, then the sole Home Page object will safely remain a singleton.

Some systems also have the ability to remove the option for anyone to create a specific type, globally (via a setting called "Do Not Show in UI" or something similar). While this has the same basic effect as removing all permissions as described above, sometimes this is available on systems with no other type restriction system. While it doesn't provide the granularity of type restrictions, it does protect the uniqueness of singleton objects.

In addition to types, sometimes we want to protect content with **attribute-level permissions**, where edit or view restrictions can be placed on specific attributes. This means the ability to create or edit a type might not give an editor access to the entire object – certain attributes can be read-only, or even removed from the interface entirely.

For example, perhaps only advanced editors should be able to change the URL Segment attribute. For all other editors, the editorial element for this attribute can be removed from the interface. Our editors assigned to a specific group would see the editorial element for that attribute as normal, while other editors might never know it exists.

Clearly, if you remove an attribute, *that attribute cannot be required.* Our URL Segment field from above would likely be auto-populated if left empty. However, if an attribute requires a value, and that editorial element is hidden from view, this is going to cause a problem.

In systems where attributes can be aggregated into tabs or collapsible panes, it's sometimes possible to apply permissions to entire groups of attributes at a time. For example, we might aggregate attributes like SEO Keywords and SEO Description into a tab or pane called "SEO Info," then restrict access to only the marketing team. Attributes added to this group should be automatically restricted in the same way.

> Does lack of access to a type or attribute in the editorial interface equate with actual permission restriction? Technically no, since the types and attributes would still be available to API access under the privileges of that user account. But, for most practical purposes, if an editor can't work with something in the UI, they can't work with it at all. If an editor is somehow able to execute ad-hoc code against the API using their user account, then you probably have bigger security issues.

So far, we've discussed model permissions around the editorial interface. But some systems extend that to their templating systems as well, which can be tricky.

Some systems have very integrated templating, where templates are modularized to the attribute level. These systems might even apply attribute-level permissions on the rendering side as well, so that certain visitors/users can't see certain information.

However, this can be difficult to manage, because templating operates on such a wide range of visual interpretation. Only very structured design systems can cope or recover from the arbitrary elimination of rendering information at request time. If any attribute can be restricted, then technically the design system has to be prepared for *any* aspect of the content object to simply not be available during rendering. This is asking a lot.

When the delivery context executes, it will know the identity of the user (even if that identify is the "Anonymous User"). When you do genuinely have a situation where a specific attribute should be hidden from a specific class of user, it's usually not *just* the attribute value that needs to be suppressed. Attribute values are normally formatted with surrounding HTML constructs, and, in most every case, those *all* need to be suppressed as well.

For instance, you may have Mobile Phone attribute on your Employee Bio type for your intranet. Access to an employee's personal phone number is on a "need to know" basis, so this should only be displayed for users in the "Security" and "Help Desk" user groups.

However, that attribute value isn't rendered by itself – there's likely a label next to it, and some container HTML construct – perhaps an entire table row. All of that needs to be removed too, but in most templates, there's no way for that arbitrary conglomeration of HTML to "know" that it belongs to the attribute which is no longer visible.

The only time this works well is when the templating and design system is deeply integrated into the content model, and each attribute somehow "carries" its own template, so the entire construct can be suppressed. You see this templating philosophy in some systems, but it's not common, and further discussion is far beyond the scope of this chapter.

In most cases, attribute removal during rendering would be accomplished in the template logic by a simple `if...then` construct that would either (1) manually check the group (for the "Help Desk" group discussed above), or (2) have access to some `IsDisplayed` property of the attribute object itself.

Type and attribute restrictions can be enormously helpful to protect the content model. Additionally, it allows some "neutering" of the editing interface to improve usability. You might find that some editors only need access to a subset of attributes on a particular type, vastly simplifying their interface with cascading benefits to usability, training, and support costs.

Evaluation Questions

- Can access to object creation of specific types be restricted by user or group?
- Can access to attribute editing be restricted by user or group? Is this individual, or can sets of attributes be restricted?
- Is validation circumvented in situations where attribute editing is restricted?
- How can specific types be protected as singletons?

Evaluation Criteria #17

How can rich text fields be structured?

As we discussed in the chapter on , many content types fit the same pattern: some structured fields around a Body of rich text.

An Article has a Title, Author, Published Date, etc., and also a rich text Body field that's the main content of the article. An Employee Bio would have the same pattern: First Name, Last Name, Job Title, and...a big rich text field for the Bio.

This is such a common pattern that a lot of systems are built around it. It's not coincidental the built-in model for many systems starts with a Title and Body field. The Title has to be there so the system could show the content in lists and menus, and the the Body was there because, well, *that's the content.*

We often don't structure the body field. It's just rich text, composed in some WYSIWYG tool, and we let editors do whatever they want in there, using whatever formatting tools available in their editor. (Which is, in itself, often a source of great debate.)

However, the industry is trending toward more structure in rich text. What used to be just a big field of HTML is becoming an aggregation of special, embedded content objects. This has considerable impact on how you might model your content.

Structuring rich text is helpful because it often removes the need for many special types that differ only in displayed elements.

For example, if your editors want a Photo Gallery Page, you might conclude this differs from a Text Page only in that an image carousel appears somewhere in the text. It might be at the top, or under introductory paragraph, or wherever, but if you remove that, you're right back to a Text Page.

Creating an entirely new type to add one attribute (the image carousel) has a detrimental effect on manageability, so it might be easier to just create an image carousel as some type of embeddable element that can be inserted into the rich text attribute already present in Text Page. In doing this, we've essentially stated *any* Text Page can become a "Photo Gallery Page." That isn't actually a real type, it's just a Text Page object in which an editor decides to embed an image carousel.

Yes, you could use type inheritance here as well – you could create Photo Gallery Page and inherit it from Text Page then add the extra attribute. However, you will run into the problem we discussed in the chapter on in that your new type can only inherit from *one* parent, and this means that you've implicitly stated your image carousel only extends *one* type of content.

By allowing the embedding of image carousel in rich text, you've creating a condition whereby *any* rich text field on *any* type can contain an image carousel. If Mary wants to display an image carousel of the company picnic she organized on her Employee Bio page, she can do that now because it also contains a rich text field. (This may or may not be what you want to allow of course, but we'll get to that.)

By the inclusion of active elements, rich text on *any* type becomes a generic container for both formatted HTML and other presentational elements. Previously, rich text was just a series of paragraphs stacked on each other, but editorial tools have advanced to the point where we can alter some items in that "stack" to be more than just paragraphs.

We call the new editor Gutenberg. The entire editing experience has been rebuilt for media rich pages and posts. Experience the flexibility that blocks will bring, whether you are building your first site, or write code for a living.

This is My Heading

Editing a section of rich text in the new "Gutenberg" editing interface in WordPress. In this example, we are selecting and inserting a new element between two headings.

Rich text gets structured in two common ways.

1. **Stackable Elements**: Some systems allow editors to "stack" elements to be delivered as an unbroken body of content. In stackable models, editors can add a "Header," for example, then a "Paragraph", then an "Image," etc. Each element is its own content type, and they stack from top to bottom. When rendered, they appear to be a complicated, unbroken stretch of rich text.

2. **Embeddable Elements**: Other systems allow "embeds" inside a body of rich text, where editors can either place (1) small text strings (**shortcode** is a common name for this) which are replaced at render time. Some WYSI-WYG tools allow drag-and-drop functionality for editors. These systems usually create a placeholder HTML construct that's replaced during rendering.

The two models are subtly different. With stacked elements, the "body" is just a container for elements – any text present is in one of those elements, and *there is no single rich text field*. The rich text is formed solely by stacking elements on top of each other, so they're not optional. If there were no elements, there would be nothing to show.

Using embedded elements, the rich text can exist without the use of any elements. Only if desired, it can also contain embedded elements between paragraphs (embedded elements are usually always block-level, for some reason though there's nothing preventing them from being inline). Think of the rich text as water flowing around "islands" of embedded elements.

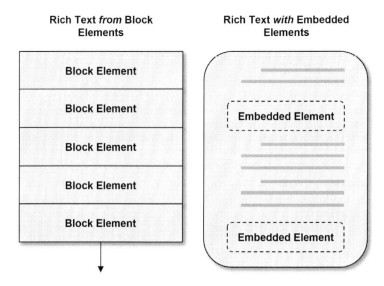

The difference between the two models of structuring rich text. The key is that with stacked elements, there is no "outer" rich text. The only text is contained inside the elements. With embedded elements, the rich text exists, but might be enhanced with elements.

Another key point is that these elements – whether they be stacked or embedded – all imply some separation of content and presentation. Many rich text editors will offer buttons and dialogs to form HTML elements, but those elements simply get embedded as their actual, final HTML manifestation. Once created, those HTML tags "forget" how they were ever created in the first place. They're the same as if you wrote them manually.

With stacked or embedded elements, the rich text field is structured from data elements rendered into HTML in the delivery context at the time of request. They are stored as a data construct, and are templated as a small, embedded content object.

An embedded element, for example, inserts some type of "placeholder" into rich text. Often, this is a block-level element that can serialize data, such as a `DIV` with multiple `data-` attributes, or containing serialized JSON. During the delivery context, the rich text is parsed, this element is detected, and is "expanded" into whatever it was intended to be.

Stacked elements are essentially content objects in their own right. There are likely a set of special types designed to stack as rich text – things like Text with Header, Image with Caption, Video Player – and the entire body of rich text is just a series of objects of these types stacked on top of one another. During the delivery context, these are rendered consecutively, resulting in a body of rich text.

Structuring rich text fields is becoming more common, and it can drastically increase the flexibility of your content model. More complicated constructs can be included in rich text, and presentational elements that would previously be modeled types which were fixed in place on specific template locations have much more flexibility

The downside is it adds some friction to the editorial process at best. At worst it can get downright complicated and tedious. Additionally, gives some editors vastly increased powers of composition, and that can cut both ways – increased levels of training and support are usually necessary.

Evaluation Questions

- Is it possible to structure rich text through stacked or embedded elements? Is this the only option, or does this exist alongside traditional rich text (HTML-based) editing?

- Are stacked or embedded elements managed content objects, or are they specific to rich text structuring?

- Can stacked or embedded elements be used in multiple rich text attributes across multiple objects, or do they exist only in the editorial space of the content for which they were created?

- If these elements can be used across multiple content objects, are they subject to dependency management or referential integrity checking?

Evaluation Criteria #18

What options are available for dynamic page composition?

There are two divergent personas of editors. In one, they create pure content and leave visual presentation up to the designers, via templating. The opposite persona is "editor as artist," where they create content and visually apply it to a page, carefully moving elements around, nudging and rearranging until the result is visually pleasing.

In reality, this is probably less about the editors, and more about the content. Both types of editors exist, and very broadly speaking, there are two types of content output – "templated" and "composed."

- **Templated content** is highly structured and meant to appear the same in all situations. It's not subjective, and editors aren't permitted to rearrange the output to suit their tastes ("Let's try the sidebar on the left this time..."). Templated content is the Diet Coke of CMS – it's meant to appear the same in all cases; its uniqueness is only in substance, not style. Example: a press release or a help topic.

- **Composed content** is visually subjective. Not only is an editor defining the words and images, but the editor is defining the *visual presentation* as well. In this case, they can absolutely put that sidebar on the right, and add other widgets and elements to different areas of the page. Composed content is the *chef's artisanal creation of CMS* – it's highly subjective and subject to the whims and tastes of the editor putting it together. Example: the home page or a marketing landing page.

Functionality to create the latter is known as **page composition** – we are literally going to "compose a page." Many systems now have support for this model of content delivery for some or all of their content.

The very idea of a "template" implies an external force (the template/front-end developer) is imposed on editors to coerce them into creating the same visual output every time – a cookie cutter, after all, makes the same cookie shape, every time. Page composition reduces this structural imposition, and transfers some of the control back to the editor.

Very rarely, an editor will get a completely blank page surface on which they can do *anything*. However, usually, they'll be granted *some* freedom of visual and compositional expression for certain content that can deviate from the standard template to some controlled degree. Where to draw this line between freedom and consistency is a key question.

Page composition can be handy for the same reasons structure in rich text areas can be handy – editors now have a palette of elements they can add to pages, which can drastically reduce the number of content types needed in your model. If they can add a photo gallery widget to any page, then you don't need to have a dedicated Photo Gallery Page type.

This sounds like the rich text structuring we talked about last chapter. And it's very similar. However, instead of stacked or embedded elements structured in a single attribute, that model is extrapolated to the larger page surface.

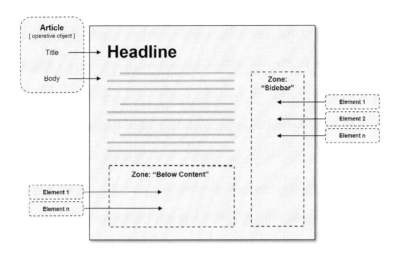

An example of a page which combines templated content and compositional content. The headline and body content are templated from Title and Body attributes on the operative content object. The page also offers two zones, into which content from elsewhere in the repository can be assigned.

Remember that, depending on the page model of the system, the zones might be attributes themselves on the operative content object.

Page composition usually operates on the model of **zones** on a page surface where editors can place and "stack" elements. Each zone can contain multiple elements stacked from top to bottom. Each element is self-contained, and renders independently of the other elements in that zone.

Elements in the zone can usually be reordered freely, often through drag and drop. Less ideally, you might see commands for "Move Up" and "Move Down" on each element.

Occasionally, elements can stack horizontally, though this is less common and gets logically tricky since the web has conventionally been a horizontally constrained medium. Some systems will allow you to specify a width on elements ("wide" or "narrow") so they can stack horizontally, while others have you add some type of **layout or column-based element** to allow other elements to be stacked inside of it.

Some elements – like the layout elements mentioned above – can **recurse**. So an element that goes in a zone, might also have one or more zones inside of it. Zones and elements can therefore become a reverse tree that renders from the outer page "downwards." In this case, the page renders each zone, which each renders their elements, some of which contains zones that render, and so on.

These zones can often be limited by type, so only certain element types can go in certain zones, and can sometimes be limited by count as well, so only, say, three elements can go in a certain zone.

Zones usually don't have to be used. What happens to an empty zone is left to the template developer and whatever HTML the zone generates by default. Usually they simply don't render at all, but they might still be surrounded by HTML constructs that leave a "gap" in the page.

Depending on the system, the same element object might be allowed to appear in two different zones on the same page, or even twice in the same zone. There aren't many situations when the same *actual element object* would need to repeat, but it would be quite common to use multiple objects of the same element *type* — multiple Image objects, for example.

Occasionally, a system might allow specific **zone assignment values**, meaning configuration values or perhaps even attribute values that override the actual assigned attribute value for *this object in this zone*. This means a single object could be assigned multiple times, with some data variation that might cause it to appear completely differently each time.

Remember that zones usually just store references to other content objects, so there are sometimes dependency considerations with page composition. Deleting an object would necessarily delete it from all zones in which it has been assigned; this might lead to unintended consequences. Consequently, most systems' dependency management will track zone assignments.

So, are these "composition elements" the same as the elements from the ? Yes, sometimes. Other times, no, they are are specific to page composition. It depends on the system.

Could we simulate the rich text structuring using a page composition zone and just stacking elements? Usually, yes. The difference is that elements used for page composition are usually independent content objects from elsewhere in the repository, and they often appear in zones on more than one object – some might exist once in the repository, but be added to every page.

Conversely, rich text structure elements are usually embedded in the containing attribute for use only in that object. Thus, they are optimized for that editing experience, and they exist and get deleted within the context of that "owning" content.

Just know if this seems confusing and duplicative, you might be right. There is tremendous overlap in systems that offer both models of structure.

The flexibility and freedom that page composition offers editors is restricted by zone existence and placement. Since editors can only place elements in zones, more zones in more places on the page surface gives them more options.

It's quite common to place zones on the edges of the page – under a menu in the left column, for example, and perhaps to form an optional sidebar on the right. Additionally, you'll often see one above and below where the main body of a content object is output, which can be used to position content elements above or below the main text – your Image Carousel could be placed above the main text, or a Dealer Locator widget could be placed below some introductory text.

In terms of number and placement of zones, consider two ends of the spectrum:

• A template might offer a single zone, below the Body of the page. An editor could write some introductory text then place an element in the zone. This would offer some flexibility in that any content type with a zone could host some "placeable" element, effectively acting as a wide variety of pseudo-content types.

• Alternately, a template might be nothing but a single zone – the HTML page would have nothing else in the BODY tag but this zone. The entire visual composition of the page would be up to editors and what combination of elements they wanted to place where. In this situation, they might just stack them from top of bottom. If they had access to layout zones of some kind, they might even form sidebars and navigation menus, and even completely simulate and recreate a more traditional page layout.

In reality, page composition exists somewhere between those two extremes. It becomes a question of editorial and stylistic freedom – to what extent should editors be allowed to visually re-arrange a page layout? The answer to this is different for every project.

However, the second scenario there also inadvertently highlights why templated content exists. Consider being confronted with a blank page surface for every single piece of content and having to hand-build the layout. *That's a lot of work*, and it would seemingly obviate the need for templates or designers altogether. Very few editors I know would want to go through this every time they wanted to publish content. Templated content exists for a reason.

Page composition evokes images of editors as artists, inspiring to create unique works of art for every page. But *editors generally enjoy templated content as much as developers*. Oftentimes, an editor just wants to publish attractive, usable, consistent content with a minimum of work.

When considering the range of page composition options, it's generally most valuable as a way to enhance selected pages, rather than it being a base feature state of all content.

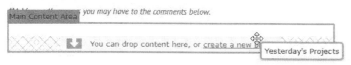

Dragging an element into a zone in Episerver (the nomenclature for that system would say we were dragging a "block" into a "content area").

What gets interesting is when page composition intersects with the page model we discussed previously. If a page is a conceptually separate thing from content, then all content is being "wrapped" in pages and that's where templating is necessarily focused. In fact, to publish a content object at all, you might need to select a page template, and perhaps map attributes to zones.

However, if the page is a content object itself, then the zones are likely just repeating attributes on a type, which means the elements become relational references from one content object to another. (One handy side effect – changes to elements and zones are likely versioned and audited as normal content changes).

Another subtle difference between the two models – with the page-centric model, the zones are likely defined purely in the template, whereas the content-centric model has the zones defined on a content type, then just rendered in specific places on the template. The difference is slight, but with the latter, there are some unique situations where you could add a zone to a content type to enter and save content references in it without ever rendering that to the page. This is sometimes helpful as an ad-hoc repeating attribute.

Some systems take page composition a step further, and let editors design a page with zones and pre-assigned content, and then *save that as a template for future use*. So, you have an editor creating a template, with dynamic zones for future content assignments, and perhaps even a "set" of content assigned to those zones, which is then stored and duplicated for future pages.

It gets a little weirder when an editor has access to recursive elements that contain their own zones. Using this, the "outer" template created by the template developer has zones where an editor can add elements which also have zones. So we have a two-stage template rendering – content is injected into the zones that the editor added, then those zones are rendered against the template which the developer created.

I don't deny there's a lot of flexibility there, but it can get complicated quickly.

Page composition is a "rabbit hole" feature. Depending on how you use it, it can completely up-end your content model. A fully composed website, where every page is a result of page composition from scratch, will have a *very* loose relationship to any underlying content model.

As a result, some very foundational decisions need to be made about how pages will be composed, and where the correct balance point lies in the range between complete artistic freedom and templated constraints.

Evaluation Questions

- Is it possible for editors to visually compose pages?
- How does this intersect with the page model of the system? Is the composition specific to an explicit page construct, or to a content type? Where do zones "live"?
- What zone restrictions/validation are possible? Can zones only accept content of a specific type? Can the number of objects be limited?
- Can attribute values be overridden for specific zone placements?
- Can zones be recursive? Meaning, can elements in zones also have zones into which other elements can be placed?
- How are zones and element placement managed from the UI?
- Can the UI support both zones specific to a content object or page, and zones that are in a more global scope, such as in a header or footer?
- Can composed pages be re-used? Can they be saved and form the basis of a further composed page?

Evaluation Criteria #19

What aggregation structures are available to organize content?

So far, we've talked about content modeling at the type level, based purely on attributes. Another aspect of structure is how multiple content objects are organized in relation to each other. This is often manifested in a content tree, but many systems offer other ways to organize content which might impact how it's modeled.

The grouping and association of content is known as **content aggregation**.

A relationship between two content objects can be referential, as we've discussed, meaning it's defined by a referential attribute or a parent-child relationship in a tree. This relationship can be said to be an **internal relationship** because at least one of the content objects knows about it – it's built into the attribute values of that content object.

Another type of relationship is an **external relationship** where two content objects are related through some structure which is external to both of them. Neither of the objects are aware they're related in this way. The external structure can be created, exist, and be deleted with neither of the content objects ever knowing it had been associated at all.

Consider a web page that links to another web page on a completely different website. In that situation, Page A knows about Page B because it links to it. That relationship is internalized to at least one of those pages.

Consider if there was no link – I just personally decided the pages were related, so I created a bookmarks folder on my desktop, gave it a name ("Pages I Like"), and put shortcuts to both of those web pages in it. In this case, my folder is the "external structure," and it imparts some aggregational value to both pages. I know those two pages are related in this way, and I know why from my own perspective. However, neither page is aware I've created this association, and if I ever delete my bookmarks folder, that relationship goes away without either page ever knowing it existed. That relationship was completely external.

When comparing internal and external relationships, the differentiating question is, does a content object have to be edited to exist in this structure? Do we edit the content object and assign it to the structure? Or do we edit the structure and assign content objects to it?

The former is an internal relationship of content, as we've already discussed. The latter is a type of structure we'll discuss in this chapter.

Categorization or **taxonomy** is an aggregational structure that allows you to organize content into groups.

From the perspective of CMS, categories and taxonomy are usually considered synonymous – it would be very rare to see both feature names in the same system. We'll use "categories" here to represent both.

> Taxonomic classification is a scientific practice with its roots in biology. Carl Linnaeus created the *Systema Naturae* in 1735 which was an attempt to categorize all known living things on Earth, and this has become knowns as "the Linnaean taxonomy."
>
> Taxonomy is a science unto itself, and any concept of "taxonomy" in a CMS is going to be a pale representation of it. In the practice of CMS, "taxonomy" is usually just a fancier way to say "categories."

Categories tend to be a "top down" system, meaning an editor or administrator has established a list of categories in advance, and when content is edited, it can be assigned to one or more existing categories. It's rare that editors are allowed to create categories on-the-fly. To create a new category, an editor would need to access an interface specifically for this, and access to this interface is usually restricted as an administrative function.

Categories are often hierarchical (a **category tree**), as it's very common for categories to become conceptually narrower and more specific as you move "down" the tree. In some category trees, a category might be marked as non-assignable and exist solely to contain child categories.

All Categories | Most Used

☐ Content Aggregation
☐ Content Modeling
  ☐ Discrete Modeling
  ☐ Relational Modeling
☐ Coupling Models
  ☐ Coupled
  ☐ Decoupled

A simple category tree in WordPress, showing top-level categories which have child categories of increasing specificity.

Your ability to search for category assignments will have considerable impact on its utility. Some common search use cases –

- What content is assigned to Category X?
- What are subcategories of Category X?
- What is the ancestor path of Category X?
- What categories is Content Object Y assigned to?
- Is Content Object Y assigned to Category X?

Does this sound a lot like a content tree? It should. The models are very similar, and – as we'll discuss below – sometimes category trees are simply formed from branches of the content tree.

With a category tree, you sometimes need to consider **implicit ancestral assignment**. If you have a tree of concepts – moving from broader to narrower as you traverse down the tree – does assignment in a child category imply assignment to all its parents as well?

Say your category tree has "Vehicles" with a child category of "Cars" which has a further child category of "Sedans." If you assign something to "Sedans," it should logically be assigned to "Cars" and "Vehicles" as well. Some APIs may support this, and others won't.

Ancestral assignment is often achieved by the ability to search for descendant assignments. From the perspective of the "Vehicles" category, it's very basic to search for all *direct* assignments of that category. What's often more helpful is to search for all *descendant* assignments, meaning all assignments to this category or any of its descendants.

Categories can sometimes hold other information besides just a name or a label. In some systems, categories can have a description, and have links to other categories, not their descendants ("related categories").

This sometimes raises the question: "should categories just be content?" Should we have a Category type, with a Title, Description, and a repeating Related Categories? And then every content object could have a repeating attribute for Category Assignments (assuming that reference is bi-directional).

If all these capabilities are in place, then this is a desirable option. The benefit is that categories become managed content. They can be versioned, they have permissions, and they have an entire editorial lifecycle attached to them. Additionally, they might now be URL addressable, so each category has a page where assignments can be listed.

On Twitter, I posed the question of whether categories should just be content objects. In addition to a lively discussion[1], Joe Miller responded with an entire article about the idea[2].

In the article, Joe applies semantics to differentiate "creating" vs. "curating" and "authoring" vs. "assembling." Some things are "of" the content, while other things are "about" the content, which is a handy summation of the debate between "content" and "metadata" that we discussed in .

1. *Twitter thread. https://twitter.com/gadgetopia/status/1145999145783758849*
2. *"Authoring and Assembling: We're asking too much from our content management systems." https://medium.com/@jjosephmiller/authoring-and-assembling-b831a2a9eb27*

The basic model for categorization is also true for **tagging**. A tag, like a category, is a conceptual structure to which objects are assigned.

The difference in categories and tags lies mainly in editorial usage. Whereas categories are top down and planned in advance, tags are often bottom up, meaning editors can create them on-the-fly. Content objects might have an attribute for Tags and editors can enter a space- or comma-delimited list of whatever tags they want to apply.

Tags

An example of tagging from the Q&A site Stack Overflow. Tags are simply entered as tokens separated by spaces (spaces inside a tag need to be replaced with a hyphen).

Architecturally, a "tag" is often just a simple text string assigned to content. Finding all content "tagged" with the same thing usually just means finding all content with the same assigned text string. There is no "central authority" for tags – a tag has no idea if other content is assigned to it. At its core, a tag is simply a "target" you can specifically search for to find similar content.

The danger of the "loose-ness" of tagging is unchecked proliferation, which can happen because there's no governing authority like there usually is for categories. What you call a "car", I might call an "automobile", and someone else might call a "vehicle". Tags will be created without any consideration to whether a similarly appropriate tag exists. To avoid this, many tagging interfaces have type-ahead suggestions or a list of existing tags to pick from.

Tags are not normally hierarchical. Occasionally, you see systems that offer a "related tag" capability, or some form of specifying an alternate tag name, so that our aforementioned "car," "automobile," and "vehicle" can appear to be a single tag.

To fix prior mis-assignments, some systems offer tag merging, where all the assignments for Tag A can be combined with Tag B, and Tag A will henceforth become an alternate tag name for Tag B.

The difference between tags and categories can be summed up by structuring and advanced planning. Categories are usually more rigid, more descriptive, more planned, and less often changed. Tags are the opposite.

You rarely see both models built into the same system. Older systems tend to have categories built-in, and tags added as a contributed plugin or module. Newer systems have tended toward tags as the default organizational method, sometimes without categorization at all.

Some systems have additional structural systems like **menus**, **lists**, and **collections**. The specifics differ, but they're usually available for ad-hoc structuring and aggregation of content.

Menus tend to be hierarchical. They often include other web navigation-specific features, like labeling, to display something other than the content's title, and hyperlink-specific functionality like whether to open the link in the same window or a new window (the `target` HTML attribute) and hover text (the `title` HTML attribute).

Lists and collections are usually just flat, ordered lists of content objects. These can be helpful for things like specifying a list of news articles on the home page, or a list of links for overhead, static navigation.

Generally, structures like these are external to the content – to assign content, you manage the structure and select the content to be assigned. Occasionally, some systems do allow assignment to a structure from the object itself.

Custom ordering is why these structures make more sense than just a "flag" attribute on the content itself.

For instance, to provide a list of news articles on the home page, you might just add a Show on Home Page checkbox to the Article type, then search for any objects with that value when rendering the home page. And this will work so long as you use some derived ordering system – for instance, you collect all the objects with the checkbox activated, then order them by Published Date.

However, in my experience, it's only matter of time until someone asks, "Okay, how do I display them in a *specific* order?" When this happens, the concept of "pulling" the articles breaks down, because now you need to store two pieces of information:

1. That the article should appear on the home page

> 2. In what ordinal position in the list the article should appear
>
> A single checkbox can't provide both of these, and the latter is logically impossible to store at the object level because an individual article has no way of knowing what other articles are designated to appear in the list with it.
>
> In these situations, an external structure like a menu, list, or collection that provides arbitrary ordering is usually the only practical option.

A pattern of tree-based systems is often to simulate these structures as branches of the content tree. Combined with the pattern of "hiding" content by not creating it as descendants of the home page, and the feature of object references, it's quite simple to designate a branch of the tree as a menu.

You could easily model a Menu Item type, with text attributes for Label Text and Hover Text, a checkbox for Open in New Window, and a referential attribute for Target Object (and even an optional External URL attribute for when you're linking to an external site). You could create an extensive branch of these objects in the content tree, then traverse it to render navigation menus.

Aggregation structures like categories, tags, menus, and lists are the utility players of content modeling. They can be quick ways to group content for usage in ways that are completely idiosyncratic for a particular situation. It's almost impossible to generalize their usage – they range from core categorization schemes, to one-off, ad-hoc content structures to populate content structures not able to be easily represented in other ways.

Evaluation Questions

- What aggregation structures exist to organize content? How do they differ from one another, and what is their intended usage?
- Does the system have built-in features for categorization or tagging, or both? If both, how do they differ? If not in the built-in model, do categorization or tagging attribute types exist?
- Can categories be organized into a tree?
- Can non-selectable "container" categories exist in the tree?
- Are their ways to specify implicit ancestral assignments within a category tree?

- How can the category tree be traversed and queried from the API?
- How does the tagging system help prevent unnecessary tag proliferation?

Timeout

What Is and Isn't Considered "Content"?

We need to take a brief detour here and talk about what is and *isn't* considered "content," in a particular CMS. And this isn't a meta-philosophical discussion about the nature of content, but rather it's a practical acknowledgment that not every piece of data managed by a CMS is the same. Some are more content-ish than others.

Consider the Article we've used for examples. If I'm a publishing company, then my articles are most of the reason I'm managing content in the first place. They're not incidental to my content model – they *are* my content model. My entire business is built around managing articles.

Therefore, we can say confidently that articles are "full" content.

What about, say, the categories I use to organize my articles? Are the categories "full" content? They have a name, and they're organized into a tree, but are they content like an article is content?

Maybe not. Depending on the system, categories might just be some data structure managed from the interface.

But, wait, isn't *everything* in a CMS "some data structure managed from the interface"? Well, yes, but some of them get more *services* than others.

Let's consider all the **services** a CMS provides to content objects:

- Full **modeling** capability, with attributes and custom validation and everything else we've talked about so far

- **Versioning**, so we can maintain a history of changes and can rollback to a prior version

- Granular **permissions** assignment, so we can control who can do what

- Some level of **auditing** or logging, so we have a record of everything that has happened to an object

- An **editorial lifecycle**, so that changes to the object are not always published directly, but can exist in a virtual workspace until ready

- An **approval** process, so that progression through the editorial lifecycle has to be approved by one or more people

- A **event model**, so that we can inject code operations at various points in the lifecycle

- An **archiving model**, where content can be deleted and removed from the UI, but retained in some form

And so on. Depending on the system, there might be a dozen different services provided around content. Fundamentally, this is what makes any particular CMS more than just a database – it "serves" and enhances content by providing extra functionality around it.

> Relational databases are formally referred to as "relational database management systems" (RDBMS) to reflect that they have their own service model which provides services around the base data they store – they have systems for user management, backup, archival, compression, querying, indexing, etc.
>
> A friend once noted that a CMS is simply a "relational database management system *management system*." An RDBMS wraps data in a layer of services. A CMS then wraps an RDBMS with an additional layer of services (described above) which are content-specific.

Our Article content object would certainly benefit from all of these services. But would a category? Does a category rise to the level where it can benefit from all these services?

In many systems, the answer is no – categories aren't *actual* content, they're just an organizing structure. They're data, but not content like an article is content.

Don't look now, but categories might be *metadata,* despite my earlier argument against the existence of it.

And when would a category cross that line? What if I wanted to model a category – provide a description and an image and some other data? Without some modeling capability (the first service described above), I don't have that option for categories, and there might simply not be a way to do that at all. Even if I could, that expanded category is now very content-like, and I'd want more services – like preview, approvals, and versioning – to manage it.

However, in most systems, there is always some dichotomy between what's full content and what isn't. Where this line is drawn depends on the system. Often, not everything managed from the interface is content, and it's important to understand what is and isn't, because editors might find themselves depending on a content service that doesn't exist ("I accidentally deleted the entire category tree... *What do you mean there's no recycle bin for categories?!*")

Some systems are "omni-content," where literally *everything* is a content object. Every type, every user, every template, every category, even every defined workflow, step, and status. These systems can get very abstract, but they do have the benefit of a uniform process of data handling which provides some level of consistency.

Unfortunately, this is rare and it depends on the development team having the foresight to build this in from product's genesis, because it can be a very complicated architecture to retrofit.

An example of evolution in this dichotomy is content files – images, video, etc. In early CMSs, these were *not* content. Usually, you just had an interface where you were managing files on the server's file system, and they were directly available to be accessed.

There was no request interception or delivery context to speak of – in fact, when a content file was accessed, the CMS wasn't even involved. When you uploaded a new file, you weren't creating a content object – rather, you were literally just putting a file in a directory on the server. There were no extra services offered.

Slowly, this changed. More and more systems began to consider content files to be "full" content objects, with some or all of the services offered to other content. We could now model file objects, and have approval workflows for them, and have code that executed on an event model. This was a healthy progression.

Not everything has *or will* progress like content files. For almost every system, there are things that are just never going to be considered full content, and never going to benefit from the complete service model. A key part of editor training is to explain what is a full content object and what isn't.

Evaluation Questions

- What is and is not "core" content in the system? What structures might appear to be content-like, but do not benefit from all the services provided to core content?

Evaluation Criteria #20

How can types be changed after object creation?

Content models are foundational. They're literally the framework on which your domain of content is built. And since every content object is based on a type, this means that some types might have dozens, hundreds, or even thousands of content objects that have been created from them.

Each of these content objects "fleshes out" the base skeleton of information that the type represents. Layered on the type's collection of attributes are the actual values, which comprise that unique object of content.

This means if you want to change a type after content has been created from it, this is a lot like changing the foundation of a house after we've built the walls and floors on top of it. If the walls of the foundation define the shape of the house, what do you do when that shape changes?

Changing a type might involve:

1. Adding a new attribute
2. Renaming an existing attribute

3. Splitting an attribute into one or more new attributes

4. Changing the attribute type of an existing attribute

5. Deleting an attribute

Adding an attribute is generally not problematic, because you have no existing attribute values to "protect." The new attribute just adds content alongside the existing attributes.

Renaming an existing attribute can be an issue, depending on the system. This is hopefully a simple operation, but some systems might never intend for this to happen. We discussed earlier that attributes have an internal name, and in some systems, this is sacrosanct and can't be changed once the type is defined.

If you *can* change an attribute name, you need to determine how these changes need to ripple through the rest of your integration and templating code. The name of an attribute is likely a unique identifier at some level, and is therefore used to refer to that attribute throughout an implementation. Sometimes, the only way to find all these references is to set up a duplicate of your production environment, change the attribute name, and see what breaks.

Splitting an attribute falls under a discipline called **migration**. A migration is the transfer of data from one storage scheme to another.

In most cases, this is accomplished using the API of the CMS to read data, manipulate it, and rewrite it back in a new format. Clearly, this will require developer support.

There's always some element of danger here since you risk leaving your content in an invalid state, but this can be mitigated by good testing and backup practices. Additionally, it's perfectly acceptable to create new attributes while leaving the deprecated attribute in place.

For example, say you have a Name attribute which you want to split into First Name and Last Name. Using the API of the CMS, you can read each Name value, split it into the two new values, and save the results back to First Name and Last Name, *while preserving the original Name*. Upon completion, you can test the result before finally removing Name. Or, you can simply disable Name and perhaps hide it from the editorial interface, preserving the data in case a problem is discovered later.

Migrations like this are normally a code-level operation. It would be difficult to encapsulate functionality like this in a UI, since the desired data manipulation could operate on a very wide range. Additionally, the resulting code execution might be a long-running operation, sometimes taking several minutes or more, depending on volume, which can be difficult to manage from a web-based UI.

Changing the underlying type of an attribute can be very difficult. Remember the actual value of the attribute is a primitive value in the underlying data storage system which is serialized from the logical type. Every attribute type is going to serialize this differently. There is *very* little chance your new attribute type will deserialize the primitive in any sensible way. If both attribute types store simple numbers, or unstructured strings, then it might work, but test this carefully.

For this reason, attribute type changes are rarely supported. Normally, you need to delete an attribute – and lose all its data – then create a new attribute with the same name.

Deleting an attribute is just as dangerous as it sounds – when the attribute goes away, all the data stored in that attribute will likely disappear immediately. And while many systems provide content versioning, *delete is still delete.*

If you delete an attribute, there's little chance the attribute will still exist in prior versions. Some systems might have a separate "archiving" subsystem from which more complete, historical data is retrievable, but since there is no longer an attribute to load that value into, this would likely be a manual recovery operation.

Some systems version their type definitions, and they will bind objects to a *specific version* of the type. So, if you delete an attribute, you would be creating Version #2 of that type definition. All of the current objects might be bound to Version #1 of that type, *which still has the attribute you just deleted.* In these case, there would have to be some utility to mass "upgrade" all objects to the latest version of their type.

While it does protect against some type change problems, this architecture introduces considerable new complexity, and is therefore rare. When provided, it's likely to be in larger enterprise content management systems.

Occasionally, you'll want to swap types – take some existing content objects, and change the type that defines their structure.

Normally, you wouldn't do this will *all* content objects of a type. If you have an Article type, then create a Blog Post type, and decide to swap *all* 1,363 Article content objects, then one has to ask why you don't just modify the Article type. If you're moving all the content objects of a type into another type, then what's the point of keeping the first type?

Usually, you want to move a *subset* of objects. So you want to isolate a specific set of objects and associate them with a new type.

Say you've been using an Article type for the CEO's blog posts, but now the CEO wants to store an attribute indicating the Mood they were in when they wrote it. You don't want to clutter up Article with that extra attribute, so you decide to create a new type specifically for Blog Post. Of the aforementioned 1,363 Article objects, there are 29 of them that represent blog posts by the CEO, so you just need to swap the types of those 29 and leave the other 1,334 alone.

The degree of problem this causes is proportional to the degree of difference in the type structures. In our example, there's no problem because our new, target type should have a matching attribute for everything on the old, source type (and one extra attribute, which will initially be empty).

Consider the inverse. Our CEO uses the new Blog Post type for a while (say, 16 more posts), then abandons the idea of storing the Mood. To simplify our model, you want to turn those 16 objects back into Article objects.

Our problem is that on those 16 objects, you now have a Mood attribute on the source Blog Post for which *no matching attribute exists on the target Article*. What do you do with it?

In this case, you can probably just throw it away since getting rid of it was the whole idea. In other cases, you might be confronted with a dozen attributes on the source type that have no "place to land" on the target type, and suddenly change our minds about switching types in the first place. Imagine a really unpleasant game of musical chairs – the music stops, and someone doesn't have a place to sit down anymore.

Select pages to convert	Policies [16537]	

☑ Convert the selected page and all subpages (of the selected page type)

Convert from Page Type	Convert to Page Type
Simple Text	Update

Convert from Property	Convert to Property
MainBody	MainBody
Summary	Summary
Section	Remove property permanently
LeftContentArea	Remove property permanently
MainContentArea	Remove property permanently

[Convert] [Test Conversion and Show Log]

The type conversion interface in Episerver. The user has selected a tree branch under which they'd like to convert all Simple Text objects into Update objects. The dropdowns for each attribute let us match off a source attribute and a target attribute. Note that two source attributes – Main Body and Summary – have matching target attributes – but three others do not, and the editor is being forced to acknowledge that they're prepared to throw them away.

Episerver allows you to do a "test conversion." It will run a mock conversion and show you the results – what objects would change, and what properties would convert. You can decide after that if you want to go ahead with the actual conversion.

Each system has its own method of determining source and target attribute matching and compatibility. The name of the attribute usually signals the intention that these are compatible attributes, and then a secondary comparison is made against attribute type.

How a system decides what constitutes attribute type compatibility is specific to the system. You might end up with some interesting values post-conversion, depending on how the new type deserializes the primitive value – for example, an image type might convert to a text type by simply storing the file path to the image.

In many cases, a "conversion" is actually a "delete and re-creation." You're not actually converting an object in place, but rather deleting it and swapping it with a new object to which you've transferred some data. This can cause some subtle issues.

Aside from the of actual attribute values, what is transferred "with" the source object in a type conversion? There's no way to generalize this, but consider that a content object has information beyond just the content encapsulated in its attribute values. Depending on the system, some of the below information might constitute additional "baggage" on a content object:

- Unique identifier

- Versioning history

- Permissions

- URL addressability

- Template assignment

- Publication status

There may or may not be parallels from source type to target type. If you try to convert a non-URL-addressable content object to one that should have a URL, does one automatically get assigned? If you convert an object that has existed for years and has dozens of edits, do you lose its entire version history?

Every system is different. You need to test for specific use cases.

In tree-based systems you might have the added complication of type restrictions.

You might have a Quiz type that *only* allows Question children. If this is the case, you'd hope the system would prevent us from turning any Question objects into Article objects, since that would violate the type constraints of the tree.

The same is true for parents. If I attempt to convert my Quiz into an Article, but an article doesn't allow Question child objects, then that conversion should be refused.

Referential attributes typing restrictions *should* also prevent invalid changes. If you have linked to an Author object from the Author attribute which enforces a type restriction, then you should be prevented from change the type of any object so linked.

Unfortunately, to my recollection, I've never seen a system preventing a type change based on referential attribute restrictions. This can be difficult because these restrictions are sometimes built into validation rules, and finding a conflict here would require identifying validation rules that might affect it, and then performing some arbitrary, isolated execution of each one.

Type conversions can get tricky for all the reasons mentioned above. They're generally something done only for significant site re-organization in conjunction with a developer, and with very recent backups standing by in case something goes wrong.

In some cases, it's not enough to just convert a type, and more complicated processing needs to be done. In these cases, a developer might just have to manually script the conversion to manipulate the data in a fully featured programming language.

When doing extensive type conversions, the only universal advice is to test, test, test...and then test some more.

Set up a parallel instance and do deep regression testing to guard against subtle effects that might surface even after a "successful" conversion.

Evaluation Questions

- What capabilities exist to change types after creation? Can attributes be added or deleted?

- Can attribute types be changed after creation? How are the attribute values converted?

- Are content type definitions versioned? Is an object connected to a specific version of the definition of its type?

- Can content objects have their underlying content types changed after creation? If so, how are attributes mapped between the source and target types? What happens to source attributes that don't exist on the target type?

- If an attribute is deleted, does its value exist in any prior versions of affected content objects?

- What information from an object is discarded during a type change? Does the object retain its version history? Permissions? Unique ID?

- In tree-based systems with typing restrictions, are these restrictions enforced when evaluating type changes?

Evaluation Criteria #21

How does the system model file assets?

So far, we've been talking about text-based content. The attribute values we've discussed are storable as strings of characters – even the ones that represent more complicated content structures.

But not everything is text, and you'll eventually need to store file **assets**: PDF documents, images, video, etc. Are these modeled as content, and if so, how does their modeling differ from the text-based content we've discussed?

> I'm going to use the word "asset" to refer to content that is centered around a file, rather than structured text. Other common terms are "media" or "content file."

The first question is whether assets are modeled as content at all. Older systems usually didn't consider assets to be managed content.

It was typical for these system to just offer an interface to manage a directory structure of files on the server's file system. Content objects could establish links to these files, and the files were exposed by the web server and directly URL addressable.

Unfortunately, this meant that assets didn't get the benefits of full content objects. They couldn't hold any other information, were rarely versioned, didn't have workflow, and usually had some alternative, simpler permission system.

Over time, in many systems, assets were slowly changed into "true" content, and now it's more common to find systems that consider an asset the same as a regular content object, and thus worthy of all the benefits of content object status. There are some differences in usage that we'll discuss below, but many systems will allow assets to be modeled like any other content object.

In addition to general asset creation, some systems allow assets to be uploaded as the value of a specific attribute. Many systems will have an attribute type for "File Upload," or something similar. This will render an editorial element as a browser file upload interface and allow a file to be specifically uploaded and stored as the value for a named attribute.

We might call these **attached assets** and **detached assets**, to represent their tie to a specific attribute.

If an asset is uploaded in this way, the asset is likely not accessible to other content and can therefore not be re-used. If the same file needs to be attached to multiple content objects, it will need to be uploaded multiple times.

This differs from a referential attribute which uses an existing asset as its target. In that case, multiple attributes on multiple objects can refer to the same asset.

In some systems, uploading an asset for an attribute will actually create a general asset, and the attribute value will be a reference. In these situations, the attribute file upload is simply a convenience and the end result doesn't differ from uploading the asset separately then referring to it.

In its most pure sense, an asset modeled as content would be a regular content object with an addressable URL and one special attribute that carries a **bytestream** to represent the actual content of the associated file. Boiled down to its essence, this is all an asset is – attributes surrounding a payload of bytes.

> File assets are often called **binary files**, due to their main content being in a bytestream, which is also known as a "binary sequence." The precision of this term is questionable, however, as technically *all* the data on a computer is represented by sequences of bytes.

An asset could have attributes modeled for when it's referenced in other content. If we wanted to display a list of assets, for example, we might include a Title, Description, File Type, and other information.

Another common use of extra attributes is for search and categorization. An image doesn't have any text for a search engine to index, so it's often surrounded by editorially supplied search terms, perhaps in addition to categorization.

We can even consider assets in terms of the delivery contexts we've discussed previously. When accessed via a URL, the delivery context for an asset would simply dump that array of bytes to the response buffer, and perhaps set a `Content-Type` header from a Content Type attribute which could be set on file upload (although that can often be extrapolated, if the URL has a file extension). The biggest difference between this and other content is that the delivery context is just passing through the value of single attribute – the bytestream.

An asset might even be "templated" in the sense that the delivery context might change what is ultimately delivered in response to a request. Variables in the delivery context (e.g., querystring arguments) might modify assets from their source form. For example:

- A specific video frame might be captured and returned as an image

- An image might be resized and returned at a smaller size

- An image might undergo batched stylistic changes; for example, it might be switched to grayscale, injected with some blur and static-like artifacts, tilted five degrees, and surrounded by a white border to resemble an old photograph

- A specific page range might be extracted from a PDF document, or a specific slide from a PowerPoint presentation

- Using machine learning, the most prominent face in an image might be detected, and the image cropped around it

- A zip archive might be opened, and a specific file extracted and returned

> For whatever reason, file asset modification is often called a "transform," a "transformation," or a "rendition," rather than templating. The words "template" and "templating" are generally reserved for text output, where static text is injected with dynamic text.

There are a few usage differences of assets as opposed to other content objects.

First, assets are accessed directly less often. Usually, they are referenced in HTML. An image is embedded with an `img` tag, or a video is referenced with a `video` tag. A PDF or other downloadable file might be addressed directly, but the vast majority of assets are embedded.

Because of this, assets usually require an addressable URL endpoint.

> Yes, I know you can inline embed images, but this is usually done for smaller, structural images (e.g., bullet points), not content images.

Additionally, assets are generally used in support of other content. This means that they need to be easily findable from the editorial interface, as they're often the target of a referential attribute.

Finally, assets commonly need to exist in the same editorial lifecycle "space" as an associated content object. If an asset is only used in support of a specific content object, it's helpful if the asset –

1. Mirrors the permissions of that object

2. Is subject to the same publishing status events, meaning it publishes and expires at the same times

3. Is deleted when the object is deleted

All of these factors combine to imply an image might be "owned" by a particular content object, which means some pseudo or explicit attribute exists to refer to that object. In some tree-based systems, the assets might be a child of that owning object, or it might exist inside a container (an "asset folder," for example) which is owned by that object.

Most CMSs aren't designed around managing file assets. It's a "good enough" feature – something a system does to check a box on a list of requirements, but doesn't attempt to excel at it. Modeling asset files is just not as important as other content to most users.

However, some scenarios are asset-centric. For example, the website for a television station might have video files as its main content type. And clearly, something like a stock photo image website will rely heavily on asset management.

In these situations, there is a specific genre of content management called **Digital Asset Management** or "DAM" (unfortunately pronounced just like it's written). DAM systems provide more tools around asset-based content.

Some common features are:

* Mass file upload (often called "intake") and object creation; for example, a photographer covering a sporting event might take 1,000 pictures they want to dump in the system all at once

* Extensive reporting capabilities

* Advanced metadata, categorization, and tagging systems

* Automatic data extraction and attribute value assignment from data embedded in the media; for example, EXIF data, from an image, or automatic textual transcript of audio

* More sophisticated physical storage options, such as near-line and off-line storage, and partitioning of logical storage

* Integration options with other systems; for example, a web CMS might be able to "delegate" all its asset management to a connected DAM

* Integration with **content delivery networks** to provide cached storage of published assets

* Advanced renditioning and transformation services (see examples above)

* AI or machine learning systems to identify subject matter in images

* In-system editing, such as image cropping and resizing, or video splicing

* Automatic watermarking or DRM embedding

These options are driven in part by the unique characteristics of the assets themselves, but also by how the different systems are used.

It's common to use DAM as a generalized, enhanced storage location. Whereas a web CMS might only contain content that's specifically published, an organization might push thousands of assets into their DAM system merely as storage, and only ever actively publish a tiny percentage of the total.

While a corporate website might have several hundred content objects, it's not uncommon for a DAM to have tens or hundreds of thousands. This makes features like reporting and tagging systems more important.

> The physical storage requirements of DAM can be breathtaking. Consider the sports photographer from the example above. With a 24MP professional camera, you can easily dump 50 *gigabytes* of raw data into a DAM in a single mass upload.

DAM systems are generally used for **media assets**, which is loosely defined as images, video, audio, and occasionally some more esoteric types, such as augmented reality (AR), virtual reality (VR), legacy formats like Flash, or source files for other rendered formats (PSD, FLA). Most DAM systems will allow you to store any file as a general bytestream.

However, for non-media files, such as text formats like PDF and Word, a genre known as **enterprise content management** (ECM) is common. Like, DAM, an ECM system is used more for storage and publication, and has features heavily tilted to reported and asset findability, in addition to an emphasis on permissions and workflow.

File assets often need modeling just like other content. They are the manifestation of the "content" and "metadata" dichotomy discussed earlier. The bytestream is the thing, and other attributes can be placed "around" the bytes in order to record additional information that enhances it in some way, or provides extra information for handling the file.

Evaluation Questions

- Does the system differentiate between asset and non-asset content objects? Do assets differ from non-asset content?

- Are inbound requests for assets handled differently than those for non-assets? Is there still a delivery context with the potential for code execution and templating/transformation?

- How is the URL for assets formed? Does this differ from the URL logic for non-assets?

- Can assets be "owned" by a content object so that they mirror its permission set and editorial lifecycle?
- Are there any built-in transformations available for different asset types that might prevent the need to store different versions of the asset?

Evaluation Criteria #22

By what method is the content model actually defined?

Throughout this guide, we've talked about building a content model as a theoretical exercise. However, in the real world, someone actually has to create your theoretical content model in an actual CMS.

How a system does this varies between two major options: UI-based and code-based.

Historically, most systems have forced the creation of a content model from the UI. Administrators could access an interface in the running system which allowed them to define new types and attributes.

More recently, **code-first** systems have come into vogue. In these systems, content and attribute types are defined in code, and the definitions exist in files on the file system. In some systems, these definitions are actual code in the native language of the CMS (a set of class definitions in C#, for example), and in other cases, the definitions are data in some structured markup language, such as XML or YAML.

Model definitions always need to be available in the repository so they can be used by the system. Models defined in the UI are created directly in the repository. With code-first systems, the definitions are in files, and the system synchronizes itself against these file definitions, usually when it starts up and initializes. Deploying a new model file will cause the application to re-initialize, perform an inventory of its existing model definitions in the repository, and change them to match the code.

If the defining code is written in the underlying programming language, then these structures are almost always used for typing purposes as well, as we discussed earlier. When template or integration developers get content out of the system, it comes out in the same structures created for defining the model in the first place.

To continue the example from above, you might define content types using a series of C# classes. Then, when templating, the operative content object is represented as an object from one of those same C# classes.

```
[ContentType(DisplayName = "Text Page", Description = "A simple
[AvailableContentTypes(Include = new[] { typeof(TextPage), typec
public partial class TextPage : BaseTextPage
{
    [Display(Name = "Title", Description = "The Title of the pag
    public virtual string Title { get; set; }

    [Display(Name = "Summary", Description = "The Summary of the
    public virtual string Summary { get; set; }
```

An example of code-first content definition in Episerver. This code snippet is a full C# class definition. We can see the content type (TextPage) with its name, label, and description; the type from which it inherits (BaseTextPage), the type allowed as child objects (also TextPage); and two attributes (Title and Summary) with their labels and descriptions.

In addition to defining the content type, when content objects of this type are manipulated from code, they will be represented by this class.

It's hard to say which option is "correct," because both have advantages and disadvantages. The market seems to be moving in the direction of code-first definitions, but there are still many systems implemented mainly from the interface and theme level, meaning very little low-level code is written. Additionally, the trend towards SaaS, cloud-based systems gives us another segment of the market where you *cannot* write any code.

Though, recently, some SaaS systems will allow model definitions from files stored in public source code repositories, such as GitHub.

Interface-based modeling does allow non-developers to create a content model, but there are some deep divisions over whether this is something that should be allowed. Content modeling requires some experience in data modeling and abstraction, and it can be easy to make mistakes.

Additionally, changing a content model usually needs to be accompanied by a change to other code or templating, so it's often just one *part* of a complete change. An administrator might be able to change the content model, but not complete their ultimate goal because they're waiting on a developer to change something else to which they don't have access. Worse, they might change the model, and inadvertently break some integration code they weren't aware of because the models now have a different structure than the code was expecting.

Remember the core principle of "predictability"? Model changes introduce *unpredictability*, with (ahem) predictable results.

Code-based modeling has the limitation that only developers can create and change the model, but – for all the reasons mentioned above – this is often an advantage in terms of security and stability.

The maintenance and deployment of programming code is known as **development operations** ("dev ops"). These are the systems and processes by which code created by a developer is stored, combined with other code, tested, compiled, and ultimately deployed to a running system (or multiple systems) in production.

Dev ops processes are mostly file-based, meaning that files are the container by which code, configuration, and other necessary data are placed into to be transmitted from one system to another.

Clearly, code-first systems have multiple advantages here:

- The files associated with a CMS project are usually always stored in a **source code management** (SCM) system, so the entire model is versioned. If you want to know when a model was changed and who did it, you can consult the SCM to see when a changed file was checked in and by whom.

- Model changes can be deployed with other code changes. When modeling from the interface, you usually have to make your changes in the development and testing environments, *then* make the same changes in production, timed with the release of new code that depends on them. With a code-first approach, you can just release the model changes with the other code and everything deploys together.

- It's easier to synchronize environments, especially during development. Model changes can be passed around as files, instead of requiring humans to identify and mirror sometimes subtle changes between environments.

As mentioned, this feature goes both ways. The "correct" approach depends entirely on the scenario, the technical makeup and sophistication of the team, and how often the model will change. The precision and portability of file-based assets is helpful to integrate with dev ops processes, but it clearly involves more development resources and configuration, and is much more valuable in developer-focused scenarios.

If a content model is not code-first, then there needs to be some other way to move model changes between environments. Clearly, a human can simply duplicate the changes via multiple interfaces, but this is inefficient. Therefore, most systems will offer some sort of **model import/export**.

From the source environment, you can trigger the creation of an export from the UI, and this would result in the model being serialized to a file, which is usually downloaded through the browser (though some systems will deposit it into a known directory on the file system, for integration with non-human processes). Then, in the target environment, you would upload that file, which would create the exported types.

Many systems allow the import and export of *objects* as well. This has nothing to do with content modeling, but in some cases, the system will include the type of every object in the export so the types in the target environment can be changed to support the incoming content.

Package Properties	Package Contents	Package Files	Pack

Content   Squirrel Notes Delete Choose...
☑ Include all child nodes

Document Types   ☐ Blog
☑ Content Folder
☑ Issue

Create of an "export package" in Umbraco. In addition to the content objects to export (the "Squirrel Notes" object and all its children), I have selected supporting content types to go in the export as well, which will be created in the target environment.

What gets tricky is if the type already exists in the target environment. If so, there's a good chance you know this and are seeking to update the type definition. In this case, how are the types being matched up? The most obvious method would be on name – if you export and upload the definition for a type named Article, this should update an existing type also named Article.

This works well, so long as source and target are aligned and kept relatively in sync. However, if the target environment has no relationship to the source environment, or the types differ wildly, then there's a chance you'd be updating an Article that has no prior relationship to your uploaded definition, and that might turn into a mess.

In other systems, type correlation is via a **globally unique identifier** (GUID) or other unique identifier, which is safer and less likely to cause disruption to an unrelated type.

This code-vs-configuration debate is really about self-determination – how much should editors be able to do without developers being involved? However, this has to be balanced against manageability, stability, and all the other benefits that a more strict management approaches brings with it.

Additionally, editors wanting to model content from the interface need to consider situations when they might want to make changes, and if the scope of those change would be confined simply to a model change, or whether the model change is just one part of a larger set of changes which extend beyond what they can complete.

Evaluation Questions

- By what method is the content model actually defined? From the UI, or from code?

- If code-first, in what language or markup are the types defined? Are these same models used to strongly-type content objects?

- What capabilities exist for model synchronization between environments?

- Are content model definitions exportable/serializable into a file? Will this file import to another instance of the CMS?

Evaluation Criteria #23

How does the system's API support the model?

Occasionally (or way too often, depending on the system) the content modeling features of a CMS come up short. In these cases, you can sometimes fall back on the system's API and use it to "code around" the shortcomings.

Our ability to do this depends on whether or not you can write code against the CMS at all (many SaaS platforms have no option for this), and to what extent. APIs vary greatly in the access and competence they provide.

Many CMSs have an **event model** (sometimes called **hooks**) by which you can attach code execution to specific events which take place inside the CMS. Some common events might be:

- Content created
- Content saved
- Content published
- Content deleted

These events usually mirror the basic editorial lifecycle of the system, and will have more or fewer events depending on specific features offered by the CMS.

There might be "check in" or "archived" events, or "move" events in tree-based systems.

To "hook," "handle," or "subscribe to" an event is to supply programming code which executes when any of these events occur. In most cases, you can insert your code just *before* the event occurs, or just *after* it has occurred. Executing code before an event usually offers the ability to change the data the event is working with.

For example, if you want to ensure that no article ever contains profanity, you could subscribe to the event which occurs immediately prior to content being saved back to the repository, and inspect the attribute values of the object being saved, changing them when necessary, and ensuring that the object saved back to the repository meets your standard.

> Poorly written event handlers are dangerous because they execute inside the expected flow of the CMS, and they can execute *often*. If you've created code that executes every time content is saved, then that code will run many, many times – even multiple times during a single editing session, as modern CMSs have rich interfaces that often callback to the server to save the content every time an editor moves from field to field.
>
> If that code has a bug, or if it executes slowly, then some Very Bad Things are likely to happen.

Before and after events are usually differentiated by name or tense. The event prior to content being saved might be "Content Saving" or "On Before Content Saved." The event after content being saved might be "Content Saved" or "On After Content Saved." For the after event, clearly you can't change any of the parameters that the event is operating on (it has already occurred, remember), but you can execute code that uses the content to affect other systems.

For example, you might want to manage your organization's tweets in your CMS. You could create a Tweet type which is not URL-addressable. Then, in the "Content Published" event, you execute code to connect to the Twitter API and post the tweet. In this situation, you gain all the benefits of managed content – versioning, auditing, permissions, etc. – but your publishing target is an external system.

Another example: let's say your CMS has no category system, so you decide to rig one up via a custom content type. You create a Category type, with a repeating, referential attribute for Content. You can edit a category and assign content to it by adding references to the Content attribute value. Using this method, it's easy for your category to list all the content assigned to it.

However, in your system, referential attributes are uni-directional. So your category is linked to content, but the content has no idea to what categories it is assigned.

You might solve this by creating an inherited, referential, repeating Categories attribute on all content objects that cannot be edited. Then, you could attach code to the Content Saved event. Whenever your category is saved, it could compare the version of the category being saved with the prior version to determine the differences, then update the Categories attribute on all affected content to add or remove the saved category reference.

This usage of an API to fill in feature gaps might be termed **model hacking**.

Many systems – especially SaaS systems – provide the ability to configure **webhooks**, which send a specially-formatted HTTP request to a specified URL when certain content events occur, such as when content is saved. The affected content is passed along with the HTTP request, and code on the other end (in an environment not controlled by the CMS) can take action on it.

Webhooks can be helpful, but they are usually post-event only, meaning they can be used to notify an external system that an event has occurred, but rarely do they contact the external system while an event is pending and incorporate any return value.

Some webhook systems send entire content objects with the request. So, when content is saved, a webhook might send an HTTP request to another system with a serialized representation of the entire content object being saved (in the request body, via a POST request). Other systems might send less information – such as just the ID of the affected content object – and require the system to "reach back" to the CMS to get more information when necessary.

When model hacking, there are two seemingly small API features that can be very helpful.

Sometimes you'll want to modify content every time it's saved. When doing this, it's beneficial to save into the *current version* of an object

Most CMSs are designed to version content, so they save a new version of content alongside the existing version. However, when updating from the API, you might create an excess of versions, which consumes storage, taxes the system, and makes it difficult for editors to isolate changes.

With some systems, you have the ability to *not* create a new version when saving from the API. Clearly, this might cause governance problems if used indiscriminately, but is helpful to limit extraneous versions and all the drawbacks that result from them.

Closely related to this is the ability to perform events "silently," meaning to selectively *not* invoke event handling code in response to events. This is helpful when writing event-based code.

When responding to an event, you might incidentally re-invoke the event to which the code just responded. This can form an infinite loop of events – saving content executes some code which also saves the content, which then executes the same code, *ad infinitum*. In addition to never finishing, this might also proliferate new versions as fast as the system could generate them.

> I saw a situation like this "run wild" in production once. The CMS became sluggish, but no one knew why for a full day until the backup process failed and the database administrator asked, "Does anyone know why the database is 43 gigabytes?" We found 1.5 million versions of a single content object. It would have been worse, but version replication had slowed down as the system ran out of resources.

To avoid this, some systems will allow you to perform events from code with the additional instruction that this event should *not* invoke other events. The event you are triggering can be executed as an exception to the event handling model.

Like saving into the current version, short-circuiting the event handlers might have some unintended consequences. It needs to carefully considered, but there are many model hacking scenarios where it's critical to writing manageable code.

When searching for content, sometimes it's easier to go around the content model completely, and simply create a **supplemental index**. This means writing content into a storage system outside the CMS repository in a format that's optimized for its intended use.

To continue the categorization example from above, let's say you've found a way to make your references bi-directional, but you might still run into synchronization problem, or have problems with finding descendant assignments. Rather than trying to keep your content model continually updated, you might just decide to go around it completely and store a representation of the category tree somewhere else.

XML is designed for modeling hierarchical structures. It has a query language designed specifically for this (XPath) and most programming languages have XML support built-in.

You could execute code on content publishing and simply write a file to the server with a complete representation of your category tree and all its assignments in an XML format designed for easy querying. In your template or delivery context, you might just read directly from this XML file rather than the repository.

And instead of keeping this file incrementally updated, you might just delete it entirely and rewrite it each time – depending on the system and hardware on which it runs, the operation might take just a few seconds, and you could likely execute your code in a separate process so the UI doesn't wait for it to finish.

A general principle holds that content systems are usually always WORM ("write once, read many"), which means we *read* from them far more often than we *write* to them. An editor might publish an article once, but it's read 100,000 times.

If you're going to optimize anything, optimize the *reading* of content, even if it means making the writing of content slightly slower.

And therein lies the elegance of a supplement index – it's disposable. By definition, the content in the repository is the "true" content, and your index is just a representation of it designed specifically to allow easy and efficient searching. At any time, you can confidently delete the index and recreate it from scratch.

Supplemental indexes are extremely common in one aspect of CMS: full-text search. Very rarely does a full-text search access the repository directly, because full-text search requires content in a specific format to run efficiently. In most cases, when content is changed, the content is deleted from and re-inserted in an optimized indexing system such as Lucene, and this is what's accessed when doing a full text search.

Repository abstraction can help by removing the need to model content at all. In some cases, a CMS's API can allow you to leave content in an external repository, and just bring it into the CMS in real-time to work with it there.

Repository abstraction swaps out the retrieval location for content. The vast majority of content will be retrieved from the CMS repository itself, but selected content might be retrieved from another storage location then converted to content objects on-the-fly for use in delivery contexts.

For instance, if your university has an extensive database of faculty members, classes, and class assignments, it would be considerable work to re-enter all this information in your CMS and keep it updated. Using repository abstraction, you might be able to make models of just the types and attributes you need, then configure your CMS to dynamically populate objects of those types *directly from the external database* when content is requested.

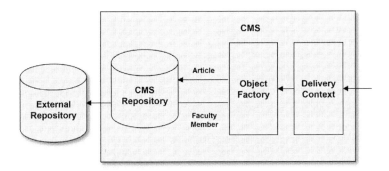

An example of repository abstraction. Starting on the right, an inbound request initiates a delivery context. To form the required content payload, the delivery context requests objects from a "object factory" to determine which repository the data for the object(s) resides.

For Article objects (and, likely, most all objects), the factory will retrieve data from the local repository. However, for Faculty Member objects, the factory will reach "out" of the CMS to an external datasource for the data.

Either way, the delivery context (and, certainly, the incoming request itself) has no idea where the content was ultimately sourced from. The delivery context is "abstracted" away from the repository, via the object factory.

Repository abstraction can be resource- and network-intensive. It requires fast, stable access to the external repository, since the CMS depends on it to fulfill active requests. However, sometimes this isn't possible or advisable. Perhaps your faculty database is on your internal university network, and you don't want to allow a constant connection to your public website.

In these cases, it might be better use **content synchronization** to automatically duplicate content from your external repository into your CMS.

In the early hours of every morning, a **scheduled job** might execute in the CMS and synchronize records from the faculty database with content in the repository. This job (1) creates new content objects when necessary, (2) updates existing content objects, and (3) deletes content objects which are no longer represented (a process sometimes called **Extract-Transform-Load** or ETL).

The resulting objects might be read-only in your CMS, or might have a set of read-only attributes if they're only partially updated from the external source. The resulting objects are sometimes called **proxy objects**, as they're simply representations or "proxies" of data stored elsewhere.

Content synchronization inevitably brings up issues of velocity and latency.

- **Content velocity** refers to how often content changes. "High velocity content" changes very frequently (i.e., a stock price). "Low velocity content" changes rarely (i.e., the privacy policy)

- **Content latency** is your need for immediacy in reflected changes. If you require low-latency, then you need content changes to show in or near real-time. If high-latency is okay, then you're less concerned about seeing changes immediately – eventually is fine.

Every decision about repository abstraction or content synchronization needs to be evaluated against the content's velocity and your tolerance for latency.

Less common, but occasionally helpful, is the ability to access the content type and attribute structure from code. When programming code is aware of itself, then it can introspect and answer questions about itself. This is called **reflection**, and the same principle works with content models.

It's helpful to be able to reflect a content model, particularly for documentation. I've been in situations where the best documentation of the content model was code that looped through all the types, all their attributes, all of their attributes settings, their help text, and all the associated validation rules, and then output a master document which served as the ultimate and final representation of the content structure.

Given that the document was generated directly from the repository in real-time, it was guaranteed to be accurate and up-to-date.

Some templating code might benefit from this as well. Say you have several content types – Article, Case Study, Analysis Report, etc. – all possessing an Author attribute. This attribute should be rendered into an author's byline, and you would like to do this in a shared header template, regardless of type. Your template code could query the type definition of the operative content object to determine whether it is one with an Author attribute, and use that information to show or hide the byline content. You could thereby use the same header template for all content, and trust that it would adapt correctly to the type of content is was rendering.

Occasionally, a system will have a **recursive content model** which means the model itself can be modeled – the model is defined *in* content.

An attribute might itself be a content object representation of an Attribute type. So, the entire model definition is made out of content objects. This means that you might be able to add an attribute *to* an attribute.

For example, if you wanted to have a supplemental search index, it would be helpful to indicate which attributes on a type should be added to the index. To do this, you might add a "meta-attribute" called Indexable to the Attribute content type on which all other attribute types are based. When assigning that attribute type to a content type, this meta-attribute would effectively become a setting that governs that particular attribute assignment.

> I wrote a case study about exactly this type of usage in Sitecore[1]. We used Sitecore to populate and maintain a pre-existing relational database from which the organization powered multiple legacy applications. These applications had no idea Sitecore existed, or that their data source was now being populated by a separate content management system.

This gets complex and abstract but some systems have decided that a content model is, in itself, *also content*. So why not manage it the same way as other content?

It's easy to fall down a rabbit hole by patching holes in your content model with

---

1. *"Case Studies of CMS-to-SQL Decoupled Publishing."* https://gadgetopia.com/post/9800

API code. Ideally, a system natively supports everything you might want to do with your content. However, in the real world, it's very helpful to have options when this isn't otherwise possible. A well-architected API and comprehensive event model can get you out of some sticky situations.

Evaluation Questions

- What is the event model of the system? Can events be captured in code? Are their prior- and post-event handlers?
- Are webhooks an explicit concept in the system?
- Can content be saved into the current version, without creating a new version?
- Can the event model be explicitly bypassed? Meaning, can an action take place that actively suppresses events that would normally occur?
- Is there any built-in support for repository abstraction?
- Are there any features design to support content synchronization against an external source?
- Can the content model be reflected or introspected from the API?
- Is the content model recursive? Is the model itself modeled?

186 Real World Content Modeling

Conclusion

Did you ever wonder why people get crazy about beer, wine, coffee, or cheese? I study cheese a bit, and I've been amazed at the heights to which some amateur cheesemongers have scaled. Some people analyze it like they're trying to get a PhD in cheese.

For others, the contemplation of wine is like a monastic commitment, and only death will stop them from their pursuit of knowledge and experience.

On the opposite side – you never find a "Diet Coke expert." No one ever bothers to study Diet Coke. They don't give any awards or titles for this.

This is because of context. Specifically, some disciplines are "high context" and others are "low context."

Context is:

> The set of circumstances or facts surrounding a particular situation.

The event of tasting wine has a lot of context. There are hundreds of inputs into that moment, from the type of grape to region of the world to the type of soil it was grown in (the "terroir") to the exact moment the grape was harvested. A glass of wine represents the sum total of hundreds of years of history, perhaps dozens of years of preparation and storage, and even the prior few moments of presentation and service. There is simply *so* much context that impacts how the taste of wine is perceived.

Diet Coke is...Diet Coke. All you can do is take a sip and declare, "This tastes like every other Diet Coke I have ever had."

In fact, Coca-Cola spends billions of dollars every year to ensure that every single can of Diet Coke tastes exactly like the last one. There is nothing to contemplate when drinking a Diet Coke. There's no mystery to unravel. It's a cognitive dead end. It's incredibly low-context.

Over the 30-some-odd chapters and 50,000-some-odd words in this guide, I hope that I've demonstrated that the practical aspect of content modeling is an incredibly high-context activity. The level of subtlety and nuance involved with making a digital representation of real-life concepts is impacted by dozens of different factors, any of which can magnify a small change and spin the path off in a completely different direction.

We like to think our ideas are exempt from practical implementation details. We have high-minded theories of our content that we're convinced will "just work" because they make perfect sense in the theoretical world of boxes and arrows we created in our favorite diagramming software.

Eventually, you have to manifest your theory inside an information system. That can be a painful reality check.

The only effective content model is one that has been implemented and has thereby suffered through the natural process of reconciling its theoretical ideal with the realities of the system in which it must operate.

I'll conclude by returning to a theme from the introduction – no system is going to do *all* of this. I don't think any one system ever could. There are architectural paradigms discussed in this guide that simply could not co-exist. Occasionally, there are simply opposite ways of doing things, and neither is wrong, they're just different.

Throughout this guide, there have been several themes:

- A CMS is a direct, practical limit on how you can model your content; everything you do will be constrained within the functional box a CMS imposes

- There is a constant tension between what is and should be built-in and what is custom – the platform-product dichotomy is a subjective balance

- A key goal of the content modeling capabilities of a CMS is to increase resiliency by protecting content from inadvertent corruption

- A CMS is instrumental in creating good content because it can add to or detract from editorial usability, and happy, confident editors make better content

- Missing features can often be reconstructed using a inventive combination of other features; sometimes, a larger pseudo-feature can "emerge" from a combination of other features

- A well-architected API can help fill content modeling feature gaps
- There is a clear dichotomy and philosophic separation between what an editor should be able to accomplish with and without development support; where this line is actually located is different for every scenario

The goal of this guide was to present a broad spectrum of features to assist in getting your arms around the solution domain in the broadest possible sense.

More specifically:

- I wanted you to think about your content model or content domain in more concrete terms, and consider how any aspect of a theoretical model might be supported by solutions actually in the marketplace.

- I wanted to help you understand and articulate the questions you might ask when evaluating a system.

- I wanted to lift the covers on the most basic of CMS features and show you some of the depth and nuance involved in their implementation.

To whatever extent possible, I hope I succeeded at those goals.

Postscript: Thoughts on Model Interoperability

If you don't care about external systems using your CMS content, or concepts like web services, standards, and interoperability, feel free to skip this chapter entirely.

I started writing this guide as a follow-up to a blog post where I had decried the lack of a "content modeling standard." I've also been banging this drum at conferences for the last couple of years.

I said this:

> [...] we need to abstract and standardize the very *idea* of content. We need to come up with a common lens with which to view content types, content objects, properties, datatypes, values, and relationships in the ways they relate to WCM.

I still think this is missing from our industry, but I've come to understand and embrace the idea that there are three "levels" to be able to share content with some other consuming system.

- **Level 1** are the tools you have to model your own content (that's what this entire guide has been concerned with)

- **Level 2** is the representation of that model which is presented to the public

- **Level 3** is the serialization and transmission method to get the data from System A to System B

As it turns out, *how* you model your content (Level 1) is no one's business but your own.

This is akin to the programming concept of "interface" and "abstraction." The content model *interface* of a CMS is what it exposes to the world, like a signature – the input and output parameters of a function. The content model *implementation* is how you actually model your content, which is the inner guts of that function which is no one's business but the function itself.

So, Level 1 is not for external consumption.

> For every perfect picture on Instagram, you never see the 50 that weren't as good, nor can you see the pile of dirty laundry just out of the frame to the left and you never know the perfect fit of that dress really comes from 20 safety pins pinching the fabric down the model's back. All you see the spectacular, choreographed result.

Level 2 is how we frame the content model for the outside world to consume. This is public face of our content, regardless of how we actually modeled it using the features of our CMS.

We could still use some standards here. We need to agree on some basic concepts. For instance, do we expose the idea of parent-child relationships? Is an object's status as a "child" of some other object a concept that an external system should know about? Is this a paradigm with enough utility we should all agree on it? If we retrieve a content object, should it be known that we can always ask for the children of it? Or ask for its parent?

This what standards like the Java Content Repository (JCR)[1] and Content Management Interoperability Services (CMIS)[2] have tried to do. Why those standards have never really taken off in the broader CMS industry is not something I'm qualified to answer (but that I wish *someone* would...).

Level 2 is essentially what we all decide to agree on, in terms of how content can exist, both discretely and relationally.

Level 3 is a communication detail. Lots of people feel very strongly here about

---

1. https://en.wikipedia.org/wiki/Content_repository_API_for_Java
2. https://en.wikipedia.org/wiki/Content_Management_Interoperability_Services

their language of choice, but my feeling is that so long as we agree on Level 2, it doesn't matter how we serialize and transmit – JSON, XML, rhyming verse, *whatever*. The concept of communicating a piece of data from one system to another is a problem solved multiple ways, and we should just let a thousand flowers bloom here.

So, to be clear, this guide has been about Level 1. Where I think we need to standardize as an industry is Level 2. Level 3 is another argument entirely, and I don't think it's a particularly necessary nor productive one.

About the Author

Deane Barker has been working in content management for 25 years. His first book, "Web Content Management: Systems, Features, and Best Practices," was published by O'Reilly Media in 2016.

When this book began, Deane was a co-founder and consulting analyst at Blend Interactive, a content management consultancy. During the writing of this book, Deane became the Senior Director of Content Management Strategy for Episerver.

He remains a founding partner of Blend Interactive.

Deane lives in Sioux Falls, South Dakota with his wife Annie.

Term Index

Made in the
USA
Columbia, SC